Living as Equals

edited by **Paul Barker**

A. B. Atkinson
Ronald Dworkin
Albert O. Hirschman
E. J. Hobsbawm
Amartya Sen
Dorothy Wedderburn

Oxford University Press
1996

Oxford University Press, Walton Street, Oxford OX2 6DP

Oxford New York
Athens Auckland Bangkok Bogota Bombay
Buenos Aires Calcutta Cape Town Dar es Salaam
Delhi Florence Hong Kong Istanbul Karachi
Kuala Lumpur Madras Madrid Melbourne
Mexico City Nairobi Paris Singapore
Taipei Tokyo Toronto

and associated companies in
Berlin Ibadan

Oxford is a trade mark of Oxford University Press

Published in the United States
by Oxford University Press Inc., New York

British Library Cataloguing in Publication Data
Data available

Library of Congress Cataloging in Publication Data
Data available

ISBN 0–19–829205–8

10 9 8 7 6 5 4 3 2 1

Typeset by BookMan Services, Oxford
Printed in Great Britain
on acid-free paper by
Biddles Ltd., Guildford and King's Lynn

for Eva Colorni
1941–1985
in loving memory

CONTENTS

Living as Equals

PAUL BARKER

Without Thomas Jefferson the idea of 'living as equals' might not exist, or at any rate not exist as so widespread, and even plausible, an ambition. Jefferson was not, of course, the first man to write about social equality. He was, partly, a megaphone for other men's thoughts, especially those of the revolutionary Englishman Thomas Paine, whose tract, *Common Sense*, was published in Philadelphia in January 1776.[1] But in drafting the Declaration of Independence, promulgated on 4 July 1776, Jefferson fashioned a time bomb which would, in due course, explode under previous ideals of social deference in country after country, beginning with the France of the *ancien régime*.

Even now it is hard to read the celebrated words and not be moved:

> We hold these truths to be self-evident, that all men are created equal; that they are endowed by their Creator with certain unalienable rights; that among these, are life, liberty, and the pursuit of happiness. That, to secure these rights, governments are instituted among men, deriving their just powers from the consent of the governed; that, whenever any form of government becomes destructive of these ends, it is the right of the people to alter or abolish it....

Reviewing Seymour Martin Lipset's recent book, *American Exceptionalism: A Double-Edged Sword*, Alan Ryan wrote that 'the thought that "the American" was a new sort of person is as old as intelligent observation of American society. Hector St John de Crèvecœur beat de Tocqueville to the point by some fifty years when his *Letters from an American Farmer* pointed out that the American lexicon was "short in names of honour and words of dignity", and that Americans might be unequal in wealth, intelligence and a great deal else, but thought of themselves as one another's social equals'.[2]

Britain had, on the surface, some of the toughest defence-works against the contagion. None the less, for at least a hundred years, in Britain as elsewhere, 'Americanization' and 'modernization' have been near-synonyms. In the novels of Anthony Trollope, than which nothing could be more English, American women feature always as wild cards: attractive, intriguing, but forever on the verge of wrecking the existing social game.[3] The two Conservative Prime Ministers who presided over Britain's full entry into the consumer society in the 1950s, Winston Churchill and Harold Macmillan, were both half-American, and proud of it.

After the Bolshevik *coup d'état* in 1917, the satirist Mikhail Zoshchenko enjoyed mocking the new, un-Russian obsession with 'Taylorism', the time-and-motion techniques of 'scientific management' that the American engineer Frederick Taylor pioneered.[4] The Soviet regime didn't adopt American-style democracy (though Soviet elections paid to it the hypocritical tribute that vice pays to virtue). It did embrace wholeheartedly the American ideal of the engineer as, somehow, the classic embodiment of the man who could do everything from scratch—the man who was, literally and not figuratively, a leveller. What was good for Gosplan was good for the country. Designers like El Lissitski had to devote themselves to trumpeting the wonders of the latest big dam.[5]

In shoving the city of Moscow into the twentieth century, Stalin, like Le Corbusier (who put in a bid to design the Palace of the Soviets), thought he would fail unless he added to his urban plans a top-dressing of glamorous skyscrapers: Manhattan on the Sparrow Hills. It is a pleasant irony that the soaring parabolic curve in Corbusier's competition design[6] was later borrowed by Eero Saarinen for his huge, arched Gateway to the West, erected in St Louis, Missouri. (Aptly, Saarinen's arch is dedicated to Jefferson.) From thence the curve was borrowed again, and doubled up, as the trademark initial M on every McDonald's hamburger joint. When a

McDonald's was eventually opened in Moscow, the symbol had come full circle.

At one level this is what living as equals now means. However rich or poor you are, you eat the same McDonald's hamburgers, drink the same Coca-Cola, listen to the same track of Tina Turner, watch the same performance by John Travolta, see the same fashion photograph of Cindy Crawford or Naomi Campbell.

In Britain, a report on the latest census noted that 'a gradual blurring of traditional demographic differentials in the United Kingdom ... has gone hand in hand with the decline of traditional institutions and the emergence of a mass culture that reaches into every part of the country'.[7] The Wearside city of Sunderland lies in one of Britain's poorest regions. It is surrounded by evidence of the decline of a shipbuilding industry that dated back to the Middle Ages, and of a mining district that went back almost as far.[8] But go into Sunderland on a Friday or Saturday night, see the high-dressing young men and women parading into and out of the bars and discos, and you have the vivid evidence to confirm the census takers' bare statistical assertion. (History is not entirely mocked. This vision of glitter and glory also falls into the long working-class tradition of The Splurge. For one high-spending week a year in, say, Blackpool, you could be anyone's equal).

In France, de Gaulle built an entire political career on an apparent defiance of American hegemony. One of his socialist opponents endorsed this rhetoric when he wrote of 'the American challenge'.[9] De Gaulle withdrew from the Nato command structure. To American official annoyance, he spoke of a Europe stretching from the Atlantic to the Urals. But what was the social reality that his rhetoric overlay, and perhaps helped make more palatable? Implicitly France went down the same track that the Federal Republic of Germany had already explicitly plunged along: to become as American as possible as quickly as possible. The Third and Fourth French Republics were the republics of *les normaliens*—the graduates of the literary and philosophical École Normale Supérieure. De Gaulle created the republic of *les ix*—the graduates of the scientific and technological École Polytechnique.

While his Minister of Culture scrubbed the dirt off France's heritage buildings, his Minister of Transport pushed motorways across the French landscape which were as powerful in creating a new France as Eisenhower's interstate highways—their transatlantic model—had been a decade before. At the edge of every French town you now see an American-style 'strip' of warehouses, stores and filling-stations, which in Europe is matched only in post-Franco Spain. The traditional French café is in steep decline as fast-food outlets open. Under Mitterrand's presidency, the culture minister, Jack Lang, tried to enforce a quota on American pop music on French radio. He failed. He ended up giving the medal of the Ordre des Arts et des Lettres (which he had recently invented) to an actress, Sharon Stone, who made her name by appearing knicker-less in a Hollywood thriller. France is now perhaps Europe's most Americanized country. When I was in Paris recently on the national Music Day (also invented by Lang), I was impressed most by the word-perfect, imitation country-and-western singers along the streets leading up to the place de la Bastille.

When the Chartist would-be revolution failed in Britain—one of the many European political failures of the 1840s—America was often the escape route. In my home town in the Yorkshire Pennines, an 'America Club' was started to help people think through, and save up for, their departure. A hundred years later, when I was growing up there, it was a point of pride locally never to call anyone 'Sir'. It was a habit I inherited. As an undeferential way of thinking it had many step-parents—religious (Primitive Methodism) and economic (subsistence farming and factories run by small masters). But I like to think that its true begetter was Thomas Jefferson. (America itself achieves an identical result in a different, very characteristic way. The social technique, always a surprise to first-time European visitors, is to call almost all men 'Sir'. This has the same outcome as using it for nobody, but you could argue that it is levelling up, rather than levelling down.)

None of this is to argue that national characteristics have been swamped. No one going to France would be misled into thinking they had landed up in some other country. In his essay in this collection, E. J. Hobsbawm notes that the would-be equality of all nations (however ill-defined) can cause much misery. It is, again, an idea with a largely American origin—in President Woodrow Wilson's famous fourteen points spelling out the principles by which a peace should be settled after the European war he had reluctantly entered. (In retrospect, by far the most important international event of 1917 took place in England, not Russia: the novel arrival on European soil of American troops. On 8 June that year General Pershing, with 191 officers and men, disembarked at Liverpool docks. On 13 June, after meeting King George V, Pershing and his embryonic expeditionary force took the steamer to Boulogne.) Yet nationalism, like the pursuit of other versions of equality, shows no sign of going away. It is an ideology of enormous power.

Everything I have written so far is cultural or psychological. Arguably, Ronald Dworkin's essay is, also. Living *as* equals is not the same thing as *being*, in all respects, equals. Notoriously, the attempt to produce this outcome results in tyranny (at worst) and administrative debacles (at best): for the first, think back to Mao's China; for the second, reflect on the muddled aims of Britain's comprehensive schools. Equality and liberty are only in opposition when either is pushed to an extreme. In his essay, Amartya Sen says that 'A dilemma is not a conflict between a good thing on the one side and a bad thing on the other . . . Rather it is a battle between different good things'.

Amartya Sen's and Albert Hirschman's essays both draw attention to the focus on the practicability of social reform which has been Italy's classic contribution to social science. Often, as Hirschman shows, this has been deeply cynical. (For the less cynical, such dry-eyed scorn none the less retains all the fascination of Machiavelli's *The Prince*.) But Sen draws from this tradition the importance of considering how a supposed reform will actually work, rather than how it will look on the notepad or printout of some adviser in all too close proximity to the men of power. Consider the disasters that expert advice has brought to Russia. Consider also, as Sen incisively does, the Maastricht Treaty's requirements for European monetary union (EMU) and their likely social impact.

A British Labour member of the European Parliament, Shaun Spiers, wrote recently: 'It seems inconceivable that the first Labour government for two decades will want to spend its first term jacking up unemployment and forcing down living standards in order to satisfy Europe's bankers.' (It is hard to believe that a successor Conservative government would be any happier; which is not to say that it won't be done by one party or the other.) Spiers added: 'There is clearly not consent in Britain for the sort of increase in centralised European power that will be necessary to control the European central bank or the hugely increased EU budget that EMU will entail. (There is not consent in continental European countries either. But that is their concern.)'[10]

Britain, like the United States, has seen a deliberately engineered increase in the inequality of incomes. William Waldegrave, a minister under both Mrs Thatcher and John Major—but not usually thought of as an ardent Thatcherite—argued for such a change in his 1978 book, *The Binding of Leviathan*, while the Conservative Party was in opposition.[11] This has certainly been delivered on.

Incomes in the United Kingdom have generally risen since 1981 but, according to the government's own figures, the income of the top fifth rose by 45 per cent in real terms between 1981 and 1992–93. The income of the bottom fifth rose by only 9 per cent, if you ignore housing costs, and by only 1 per cent if you include them.[12] You can see the evidence in the streets of any city, or in the grim housing estates, sodden with unemployment, on many of the outskirts. In London especially, the contrast between the glossiness of the many and the shabbiness of the few gives daily evidence of the gap—or it would but for the fact that the few walk or catch a bus, while the many drive past in their cars. A. B. Atkinson's essay suggests how this shameful social division can be made more visible in political debate.

Whether any collective enterprise, ever again, will be attempted by a British government on the scale of the National Health Service may be doubted. Dorothy Wedderburn shows what a remarkable story it is, in spite of all the ups and downs since its creation. Infant mortality continues to fall. Life expectancy continues to grow by about two years every decade. The health service has played a part in both these achievements (though so have prosperity, housing and education). It has had to live with the complications brought about by its successes. (Any reform is always the beginning of the next problem; which is not an argument against reform.) More frail children and more frail old people both mean more demands for health care. As older diseases fade (rickets), others arrive (AIDS). Nor did the architects of the service ever foresee the other, sometimes bizarre calls that would be made on it. (Cosmetic surgery to remove tattoos became, at one point, the most notorious example.) We must be grateful that they did not. The Iron Law of Unintended Consequences has its good side as well as its bad. The greatest achievements are due, sometimes, to those who don't know exactly what they have begun.

Throughout the half-century of its existence, the NHS has helped people to feel that they can hope to live as equals in at least one zone of British life. When people are asked which professionals they place most trust in, doctors come top of the list.[13]

Paradoxically, however, part of the pressure on the health service comes from the fact that the circumstances in which it was created have now changed so drastically. Mass culture has brought a new psychology of consumption which is both libertarian and egalitarian.

In the Britain of the mid-1940s the evidence of the Poor Law still lay all around. The workhouse had been abolished but the buildings were still there. The fear of it remained. (My mother remembered inmates of the local workhouse coming into town on their permitted day out, their clothes marked with a special patch, like concentration-camp captives.) Some of the early NHS infirmaries were former Poor Law institutions. The old and senile lay in the same beds under the same tall, narrow windows, but these were now 'geriatric wards'. In Inner London I know of at least one former workhouse where a major teaching hospital still has wards. But mass culture brings other, less humble attitudes. Users now expect hospitals to be as efficient in allocating beds as airlines are in booking seats. They want a 'front of house' as welcoming as a Center

Parc holiday resort, not a tacky reception desk where they are supposed to be grateful for the least flicker of attention.

This collection of essays has its origin in a series of lectures given in London in honour of Eva Colorni, who was passionate about the constant need for greater equality.* Living as equals isn't a race with a single finishing post. It is a moving target. 'How is it', Dr Johnson asked in a High Tory pamphlet,[14] 'that we hear the loudest yelps for liberty among the drivers of negroes?' Even the Declaration of Independence didn't mean independence for everyone.

---

* See Amartya Sen's introductory essay, and the observations on pages 143 and 145.

Social Commitment and Democracy: The Demands of Equity and Financial Conservatism

This essay is concerned with a conflict—or an alleged conflict—that is quite central to contemporary social and economic policy, and which has a particular relevance to ongoing political debates in Europe. This concerns the tension between the public commitments of the society, on the one hand, and the need for financial prudence, on the other. The commitments of a modern society to its members (especially the less fortunate citizens such as the poor, the ill, the old, and the unemployed) are recognized to be broad and important, but honouring them fully can involve heavy economic costs, and thus raise questions of financial stability and economic viability. Those who emphasize extensive social commitments, therefore, clash regularly with others who give priority to financial prudence and caution (particularly in the form of severe reductions of budget deficit and the limiting of public debts). How should we think about this conflict and weigh the contending concerns?

These tensions have been manifest for a long time now in the political economy of the contemporary world—both in the rich countries and in the poor ones—but they have acquired particular topicality at this time because of recent political developments. The salient events include political confrontations in many countries in the world today, perhaps most prominently in France, but also elsewhere in Europe, including Germany and Italy. In fact, in one way or another, virtually every country in Europe is involved in this conflict—from Ireland, Britain and Sweden, to countries in the former Soviet Union and East Europe. There is also a serious confrontation in America, as the battle lines are redrawn between liberal Democrats and radical-right Republicans. Moving further, we find very similar disputes involving the respective roles of social commitment and financial conservatism in the poor countries as well: in Asia, Africa and Latin America. Telling examples of a confrontation of ideas can be found plentifully in different countries across the world. The social conflict I want to discuss is as 'global' an issue as any that demands our critical attention at this time.

A personal note

Before I proceed further, however, I should say something about the particular occasion for this collection of essays, which are (with the exception of this one) based on the Eva Colorni Memorial Lectures given at London Guildhall University. Eva Colorni, my late wife, who was born in Italy on 7 April 1941 died from cancer, at a young age, eleven years ago in London. I have been asked to write something about the themes of this volume, taking note of the way Eva saw these issues.* I appreciate this opportunity, even though it is deeply disturbing to try to see a loved person as disembodied thought, or to concede, once again, the power and finality of the terrible event that occurred more than a decade ago.

Eva wrote rather little herself, but her friends will remember her engaging and penetrating conversations, arguing forcefully for some positions, and disputing others. Her internationalism com-

---

* Eva would have been, I think, pleased with this collection, including the choice of themes. She would have liked to have read the essays—on some of her favourite themes, by some of her favourite people. She took much pleasure in reading, whenever she could find time in her busy life of teaching, designing, wood-working, mothering, and other activities. One of my cherished memories is that of her radiant face underneath a decorated lamp, or next to a bright window, manifestly captivated by what she was reading—with tell-tale signs, respectively, of enjoyment, agreement, astonishment, anger, or disbelief.

bined well with her ability to feel quite at home in several different countries, including India and Britain, in addition to her native Italy. While this quality was partly instinctive, it was also governed by her intellectual non-parochialism, which made her treat national-ity and community as almost accidental features of a person.

Eva also had a spontaneous as well as reflective aversion to inequality, and this was an important part of her deep involvement in the political, social and economic concerns of the contemporary world. Her social beliefs included a general conviction of the need for equality, along with a more specific commitment to the interests and freedoms of the least advantaged in the society.* Indeed, she took this to be the most important aspect of equity; one on which she was frequently vocal. In the political positions she took, the direction of her sympathy would be absolutely clear and predict-able, even though the content of her proposals would sometimes be very hard to anticipate, because of her insightful causal analysis.

There are two aspects of her intellectual commitment to which this essay particularly relates. First, one of the distinguishing features of her causal concerns was her great interest in how things *actually* work out, as opposed to how they are 'meant' to work out. She was at home with actual political processes, and had much scepticism of proposals to do good based on the 'best-case scenario'. Even the demands of equality, central as they were in her thought, could not be seen in purely abstract terms, or translated into instru-mental proposals on the basis of imagined, or wishful, relations.

Second, on many of the social dilemmas, her position was more firmly procedural than imperiously substantive. When there is a conflict between two demands each of which seems important, her democratic inclination would be to look not only for how she would balance the two concerns (important though it is to do this) but also to try to see what balance would emerge from a truly

---

* In her lecturing career at Delhi University and at the City of London Polytechnic (now, London Guildhall University), her involvement with disadvantaged students was quite striking, and it was, therefore, particularly pleasurable—though unsurprising—that when the Eva Colorni Memorial Trust was set up after her death, a great many small contributions came from her former students, some of whom were quite hard up themselves.

democratic process. In this sense, she engaged herself less like a policy boss in Whitehall or in the White House (as many economists clearly do), and more like a political perfectionist looking for the outcome that would emerge from open discussions, debates and consensus. It was not just a question of balancing people's conflicting interests (as a 'Government House utilitarian' might do) but also of looking for democratic solutions based on political participation. This principle of participation was as important for her as was her determination to look for realism and actuality in pursuing the goals to which she felt committed, which included (as already mentioned) a deep belief in equality, particularly in the form of giving priority to the least advantaged.

I shall presently try to relate these aspects of her belief system to the contemporary debates in Europe and America, and in particular to the conflict between social commitment to the weak and the deprived, and the economic prudence of financial conservatism. The applications are not Eva's, though I believe she would have listened to them with some sympathy, and noted their relation to her own concerns.

The background of Italian participatory politics

Eva's commitment both to equity and to genuine political processes (including the need for realism as well as for participation) related to her own family background and the traditions of socially conscious politics in Italy. Her family background included much political action along with far-reaching social and political visions.[1]

Eva's father, Eugenio Colorni, who was a distinguished philosopher (and worked on political philosophy as well as epistemology and the philosophy of science), was also involved in active politics, and wrote both about basic ideals and about what can be done here and now. He also dedicated himself to anti-Fascist movements in Mussolini's Italy, and was very active in the resistance. He was imprisoned in 1938, sent to the island of Ventotene, and then held in detention in Melfi. When he managed to escape, he joined the underground and helped to reconstitute the Socialist Party and edited its journal *Avanti* (then clandestinely published), and was ultimately killed by the Fascists, in late May 1944, just a few days before the Americans reached Rome.

Eva was then a small child, and was brought up by her mother, Ursula Hirschmann (a committed socialist and internationalist herself),[2] and by her stepfather Altiero Spinelli. Spinelli was also in the resistance and was imprisoned for many years, with a long stint in the same island of Ventotene. Spinelli's political commitments involved early left-wing activism, particularly as a member of the Italian Communist Party, which he joined in 1924 at the age of 17, and from which he was expelled by hardline party leaders in 1937, essentially for his democratic inclinations. He continued his anti-Fascist activism outside and inside prison, and was later one of the prime-movers of Partito d'Azione (the successor of the movement called 'Giustizia e Libertà' and clearly the most liberal wing of the anti-Fascist movement).* He was a founder of the European Federalist Movement, writing—with Ernesto Rossi and in collaboration with Eugenio Colorni—the 'European Federalist Manifesto' in 1941 while imprisoned in Ventotene, and officially establishing the new Movement in Milan (again in the company of Colorni and others) on 27 August 1943. The emergence of participatory democracy at the widest level was an important part of the hoped-for European community.

As is widely recognized, Spinelli did a lot of the intellectual fathering of the union of Europe. Spinelli did live to see the birth of the European union, influenced its evolution, and, for a while, also served as a Commissioner of the European Community. As a pioneering theorist of European unity, Spinelli was concerned not only with foundational ideas but also with its actual operations. For

---

* Even though Colorni and Spinelli were on the same side on most political issues, Colorni refused to join the Partito d'Azione, largely on grounds of its élitism and its inability to involve the masses. The first Prime Minister of liberated Italy was Ferrucio Parri, a leader of the Partito d'Azione, but he lasted only a few months. The lack of a popular base reduced the effectiveness of the party, which was ultimately dissolved in 1947.

example, the endorsement by the EC of the 'principle of subsidiarity' (much under discussion right now), in the 1984 Draft Treaty on European Union, was prepared by the European parliament at the initiative of Altiero Spinelli, then a leading member of that parliament.[3]

Commitments and conflicting concerns

The prevailing political and social values with which Eva grew up were not just those of ideals and objectives but also of serious interest in ways and means, especially in participatory politics. If I were to characterize Eva's approach to egalitarianism, I would see it as a combination of an unwavering commitment to the idea of equity, with a robust realism and a strong belief in the importance of democratic political process. It was 'practical reason' in a rather direct and material sense, and was much in line with what Eugenio Colorni and Altiero Spinelli had described in their jointly authored 1941 'Manifesto'.

Egalitarianism can take the form of an abstract ideal and involve lofty sentiments, and it would be maimed as a moral and political principle if it were to be deprived of that connection. However, egalitarian priorities can be used in a variety of ways, with diverse relations to realism and veracity. There is, on one side, the moving prose of a Rousseau or a Godwin, with a rather modest interest in the details of how the world actually works (including the powerful influence of economic incentives, political constraints, administrative abuse, and so on). These important works contribute to the motivation and resolve that make people search for egalitarian arrangements. And yet there is a major gap at the level of practice and action between those precepts and the political and economic arrangements for ownership and taxes, social security and safety nets, and economic initiatives and political regulations. The choice of such arrangements has to be deeply sensitive to a realistic understanding of the world in which we live.

There are many conflicting concerns in the pursuit of equity. Perhaps the most discussed is the conflict between distributional equity and aggregative concerns. The need for incentives may be rightly seen as including an element of blackmail. It would typically include the claims to higher reward for the better endowed and the more productive, who can decide to do less of those of their activities that benefit others, unless they receive more 'compensation'. If this connection does actually work this way, then an uncompromising pursuit of equality may be self-defeating. Blackmail or not, the incentive connections must be taken into account by someone trying to promote equality.

Another conflict relates to regulations that, if properly implemented, would do much to promote general equality, but which can create unintended disparities through administrative abuse. If scepticism is now rampant about a variety of egalitarian instruments varying from 'affirmative action' to 'targeted assistance', the recognition of practical limits of administrative optimality clearly has much to do with it.

Still another conflict is that between the need for raising minimal wage rates to give the people involved decent living standards, and the employment-restricting effects that doing this through legislation might sometimes have. Various compromises are possible, varying from proposals guaranteeing a basic income to all to subsidies for employing those who would not otherwise be employed.[4]

Other such conflicts can be identified related to the implementation of the basic ideals of equity. Much would depend on how the basic ideals are pursued, and how the actual impact of the respective policies are to be taken into account.

Egalitarian commitment and financial prudence

As was mentioned earlier, this paper is concerned primarily with one such conflict, or apparent conflict: that between the social commitment of a society to equity (including providing support for those who would be otherwise miserable and deprived) and the need for economic prudence and financial conservatism in not indulging in public overspending.[5]

Is this a real dilemma? More generally, what makes a decision problem a real dilemma? A dilemma is not a conflict between a good thing on the one side and a bad thing on the other, with problems in making sure that the former wins over the latter. Rather, it is a battle between different good things, each of which commands our attention, but which are in tension with each other. We cannot hope to resolve a genuine dilemma by just dismissing one side of the case in favour of a total victory of the other. A social dilemma, like personal ones, takes the form of what John Dewey, the American philosopher and educationist, called a 'struggle within oneself'. 'The struggle', as Dewey put it, 'is not between a good which is clear to him and something else which attracts him but which he knows to be wrong'. Rather, 'it is between values each of which is an undoubted good in its place but which now get in each other's way'.[6] If a private dilemma is a struggle within an individual, a social dilemma is one between different values each of which command public concern and can reasonably compete for our respect and loyalty. The subject matter includes tensions between respective demands made on the society by conflicting principles that cry for our attention.

If this is the right way of thinking about a social dilemma, then the first thing to do is to examine what these values are that conflict with each other, and why they are accepted as valuable in the first place. Why do we accept that there are social commitments—for example, to the poor, to the unemployed, to the ill—that a just community should honour? How far should these commitments extend? Similarly, why is financial conservatism taken to be worthy? How should we judge the merits of something which communicates much less readily than the need to help the deprived? What would go wrong if we departed from financial prudence? It is only after these more preliminary issues have been discussed that we can go on to address the problems raised by the *conflicts* between these quite different types of values.

Social commitment of a contemporary society

Let us first consider social commitment. The twentieth century has seen a deep undermining of the idea that individuals alone are responsible for their own predicament. The idea of a minimalist state, which is responsible for law and order and not much else, has been persistently rejected over the last century. There have been, to be sure, forceful presentations of conservative libertarianism, but the appeal of such minimalism has tended to be confined to the periphery of national politics in most countries in the world. The idea of a 'welfare state' has gained acceptance, at least in principle, through much of Europe and North America, and also in Japan and increasingly in the newly successful economies of East Asia. Even in some very poor economies, with quite different political systems, such as China, Sri Lanka, Costa Rica, Jamaica, and the Indian state of Kerala, particular civil obligations in providing health care and social security have been accepted widely as a necessary social commitment, and they have reaped as they have sown, with high life expectancy and other achievements in enhancing the quality of life despite poverty.[7]

Even though socialist economies, including those led by Communist parties in different parts of the world, have been riddled with economic and political problems (and oppression too), the *aims and objectives* that made socialism appeal to people remain just as relevant today as they were half a century ago. Conceptions of social justice have persistently resurfaced after being undermined by difficulties encountered by particular proposals of implementation.

Interdependence and mutual obligations

Why this resilience? The foundational appeal of social commitment is not hard to explain. A society involves interaction, and our lives depend on each other. As John Donne put it, almost four centuries

ago, 'No man is an *Island*, entire of its self'. The idea of mutual de-
pendence cannot but point towards mutual responsibilities. There
is, I think, nothing particularly mysterious in the recognition that,
just as members of the society benefit from interaction with each
other, they must also accept deep-rooted obligations to each other.

The basic idea of obligation towards each other in a given society
is not new. Even the concept of a 'categorical imperative' developed
by Immanuel Kant two centuries ago reflects affirmative acceptance
of such obligations towards each other. However, what are taken to
be the 'spheres' of social obligation and commitment have grown
very substantially since the time when Kant was writing. Why has
this happened? This is a development in which both capitalism and
socialism have made substantial contributions.

Capitalist development and social commitments

With the emergence and expansion of capitalism, the extent of
social interdependence and interaction has steadily grown in modern societies with the rapid expansion of economic exchange and
social intercourse. If no one looked like an island to John Donne
four centuries ago, people are much more closely interwoven with
each other in the world in which we now live. With growing
interdependence, it has been natural to think of expanding commitments to each other. Even though, in principle, capitalism is
ruggedly individualistic, it has, in practice, contributed to that
integrating tendency because of the way it has made our lives more
and more interdependent. Furthermore, the unprecedented expansion of general economic prosperity that modern economies have
brought to the world makes it feasible to accept social obligations
that simply could not be 'afforded' earlier on.

Ideologues who champion the 'spirit of capitalism' may be very
hostile, as they often are, to the idea of commitments of the society
or the state. But the growth of capitalism itself has contributed
plentifully to the remarkable increase in the accepted domain and

scope of social commitment in general, and of the responsibilities of the state and civil society in particular.

Socialist questions and political relevance

A second contributing factor has been the growth of socialist critiques of capitalism, related to inequalities and disparities that characterize even the most prosperous of societies. The socialist movements that germinated in Europe in the nineteenth century, and gathered strength across the world, have drawn on the observation that social and economic change can bring remarkable prosperity to some without that prosperity being shared by others. While many of the *means* that socialist movements particularly favoured, including state ownership of means of production, have proved to be both less effective and less workable than was anticipated, the recognition of the need to pay attention to inequalities and deprivations has not diminished. The socialist solutions may have been rather seriously undermined, but the socialist questions which build on discontent with the inadequacies of capitalism continue to be asked with much force.

Indeed, critiques of capitalism have, to a considerable extent, become *more* widely shared after their dissociation from the particular institutional remedies traditionally championed by socialists. There is no longer any need to swear loyalty to particular institutional proposals—be it 'nationalization of means of production', or 'state control of investment activities'—to assert the need for remedying inequity and deprivation. Much more attention is now paid to the fact that different social, political and economic arrangements can be combined with basically market economies, with different commitments to the less fortunate within a generally capitalist system. Emphasis on social responsibility can now go with a free search for means; for whatever way that might be practically most effective. The questions that socialists asked have grown even as the answers that socialists traditionally gave have shrunk.

We cannot escape the idea of social responsibility, no matter where we stand in terms of our favourite remedy for injustice and misery. Even though barriers between nationalities and communities have often been extremely divisive (indeed these divisions have sometimes erupted into senseless violence), the idea of extensive social commitment to all citizens within a nation state has been hard to overlook in the contemporary world. Even those who have argued for severely limiting the role of the state in helping the deprived within a nation state have typically found it difficult to question the goals that motivate these social commitments. They have tended to concentrate, instead, on the conflict between catering to these commitments and other concerns: incentives, red tape, corruption, ineptitude, arbitrariness, and so on. And most relevantly for the topic of this paper, there is the tension between public expenditure to meet these social objectives and other obligations of the state, particularly economic viability and political stability.

Individual freedom as a social commitment

The domain of what is taken to be social commitment has varied from society to society. To some extent this has been connected with the idea of what a country can 'afford'. A poor economy may not be able to provide the guarantees for its citizens that a rich country can. In the specific context of West Europe and North America, the commitments emphasized have included some guarantee of basic health care, protection from abject poverty, insurance against unemployment, provisions for the disabled and the infirm. Commitments have also been recognized in the fields of educational expansion (and the related need for research and development), on which the economic progress of a nation may substantially depend. The possibility of coverage links with the question of financial prudence and economic viability, and I shall come back to this issue later on in this essay.

Some of the most important social commitments are, in fact,

much broader than what can be called 'socialist' commitments in any obvious sense, even though many socialists had put much emphasis on them. If there is one general theme that can be identified as the overarching social commitment that commands our attention in the contemporary world, it is the importance of individual freedom, in the broadest sense, as a shared condition of living. I have tried to discuss the domain and implications of this commitment elsewhere (in an essay entitled 'Individual Freedom as a Social Commitment').[8] The content of individual freedom includes, on the one hand, those positive and enabling facilities that make it possible for us to function as viable and responsible individuals, including essential health care, basic education, freedom from hunger and intense deprivation, and so on. It also includes, on the other side, our basic liberties and autonomies, and the freedom and opportunity to participate in political and social processes that affect our lives. Freedom is valued in this framework both in its negative and positive sense.[9]

Participation and social commitment

The freedom to participate is very central to the social dilemma with which this essay is concerned. The opportunity to participate in the decision-making process that determines the balance between social commitment and financial prudence is itself a part of the most elementary social commitment that has to be acknowledged. In balancing the conflicting claims of divergent principles, an adequate understanding of these principles and their implications is essential, and this cannot be achieved except through wide and participatory discussions.

There are many things that we might have good reason to value if they were feasible, and the choice of priorities is inescapably a judgemental exercise in which participation of the different groups involved in these conflicting claims is a basic necessity. The central social commitment has to include the elementary rights of participation that make it possible for citizens to interact and to decide on values and priorities. I would argue that one cannot begin to understand the confrontations in the contemporary world—whether in Britain, France, Germany and Italy, or in the United States, or in China and India—without assessing them in the perspective of valued participation.

The real case for financial conservatism

Before I pursue that line of reasoning, let me move to the other side of the social dilemma under examination, namely the importance of economic prudence and financial conservatism.[10] It is tempting to think that the point of financial conservatism is the simple and conspicuous compulsion of living within one's means. As Mr Micawber put it rather eloquently in *David Copperfield*: 'Annual income twenty pounds, annual expenditure nineteen nineteen six, result happiness. Annual income twenty pounds, annual expenditure twenty pounds ought and six, result misery.' That analogy with personal solvency has been powerfully used by many financial conservatives.

In the case of the state, as opposed to an individual, this argument is not fully appropriate. The issue, for most states, is not really solvency, but the social costs of financial over-indulgence. Unlike Mr Micawber, a state can *continue* to spend more than it earns through borrowing and even through expanding the printed money supply. The real issue is not whether this can be done (it certainly can be), but what the *effects* of financial overspending might be. The basic issue to be faced, therefore, is the consequential importance of macroeconomic stability. The case for financial conservatism lies in the recognition that price stability is very important and can be deeply threatened by fiscal indulgence and irresponsibility.

What, then, is the evidence that shows the pernicious effects of macroeconomic instability—of inflation in particular? In a forceful, critical survey of international experiences in this area, Michael

Bruno notes that 'several recorded episodes of moderate inflation (20–40 percent [price rise per year]) and most instances of higher rates of inflation (of which there have been a substantial number) suggest that high inflation goes together with significant negative growth effects'. And 'conversely, the cumulative evidence suggests that sharp stabilization from high inflation brings very strong positive growth effects over even the short to medium run.'[11] Here, in short, we begin to get one rationale of financial conservatism.

Danger zones and dynamic instability

This reasoning too is not exactly straightforward, since Bruno also finds that 'the growth effects of inflation are at best obscure at low rates of inflation (less than 15–20 percent annually)'. He goes on to ask the question: 'why worry about low rates of inflation, especially if the costs of *anticipated* inflation can be avoided (by indexation) and those of *unanticipated* inflation seem to be low?'

The real case for financial conservatism lies in the dangers of ignoring caution and the possibility of escalation. There are the serious prospects of 'dynamic instability' here. As Bruno notes, 'inflation is an inherently persistent process and, moreover, the degree of persistence tends to increase with the rate of inflation.' Bruno presents a clear picture of how such acceleration of inflation takes place, and makes the lesson graphic with an analogy: 'chronic inflation tends to resemble smoking: once you [are] beyond a minimal number it is very difficult to escape a worsening addiction.' In fact, 'when shocks occur (for example, a personal crisis for a smoker, a price crisis for an economy) there is great chance that the severity of the habit . . . will jump to a new, higher level that persists even after the shock has abated', and this process can repeat itself. This is, of course, a quintessentially conservative argument, and a very persuasive one, based as it is on a rich set of international comparisons.

This, then, is the central case for financial conservatism, and it is not hard to see that this principle might well conflict with the demands of extensive social commitments of the government and the civil society. I shall examine that issue more, but before that I would like to distinguish between the real demands of financial conservatism and the interpretations that are put on it in many political arguments.

Anti-inflation and anti-deficit radicalism

Financial conservatism is *not* a demand for what can be called 'anti-inflationary radicalism', with which it is often confused. The case made is not for eliminating inflation altogether, irrespective of what has to be sacrificed for that end. Rather, the lesson is to keep in view the likely costs of tolerating inflation against the costs of reducing it, or of eliminating it altogether. The critical issue is to avoid the 'dynamic instability' that even seemingly fixed chronic inflation tends to have, if it is above a low figure. The policy lesson that Bruno draws is: 'The combination of costly stabilization at low rates of inflation and the upward bias of inflationary persistence provide a growth-cost related argument for keeping inflation low even though the large growth costs seem to be directly observed only at higher inflations.' The thing to avoid, in this argument, is not just *high* inflation, but—because of dynamic instability—even *moderate* inflation. But radicalism in the cause of zero inflation does not emerge here as the appropriate reading of the demands of financial conservatism.

Something similar can be said about 'anti-deficit radicalism', which too is often confounded with financial conservatism in contemporary debates. This clouding of distinct issues is seen clearly enough in the ongoing debate on balancing the budget in the United States. Recently, parts of the US government have been repeatedly shut down in the battle between the two parties, namely the Congress and the President, involving wrangles that closely relate to this question.

US deficit and balanced-budget radicalism

The US budget deficit is indeed large, and the case for reducing that deficit is certainly strong, given the huge burden of the national debt and its escalation. However, after accepting that general point, we must also put the matter in proportion. The US budget deficit may be large but, as a ratio of the national income, it is the smallest among the seven leading industrial countries of the world (the members of the so-called G-7), and unlike them meets the Maastricht criterion of having a net borrowing ratio of less than 3 per cent of the GDP (gross domestic product). Also, the budget deficit as a proportion of the GDP, which is less than 2.5 per cent at the time I write this, is considerably smaller now than it used to be (indeed about half of what it was only a few years ago).[12]

If it is reasonable enough to demand, nevertheless, that the deficit should come down further, this is hardly the same as an overarching need for a rapid rush to zero budget deficit, which is what the new majority in Congress tried to impose on the government. In fact, President Clinton promised to do this in seven years, and in this respect the Republican majority got a crucial concession from the US administration, even though it wanted more.

This is a victory for balanced-budget radicalism and must not be confused with financial conservatism in any obvious sense. While financial conservatism must tend to demand that a reduction in US budget deficit takes place reasonably fast (for fear of the habit-creating effects of which Michael Bruno speaks), this is not at all the same thing as the necessity of eliminating budget deficits *altogether* within a few years, no matter what the social cost of this might be. There is not much of a strong inflationary pressure in the US economy at the present time, and the economic situation would not seem to be anywhere near the prospect of dynamic instability identified by Bruno. The items to be axed in the proposed balanced-budget exercise include several programmes on which the well-being of many of America's poorest rather crucially depends. To depart altogether and quite suddenly from the past (including the tradition of assistance to the needy that is well established in America as a part of social commitment) can scarcely be seen as conservatism of any kind. It is clearly a *radical* departure: a case of anti-deficit radicalism.

European inflation and unemployment

Europe too has gone through such radicalism over the recent decades. Radicalism of monetary and fiscal policy, masquerading as conservatism, can be seen in the insistence on policy packages that give nearly complete priority to the avoidance of inflation (a priority formalized by many central banks in Western Europe), while tolerating remarkably high rates of unemployment, which are seen as necessary costs to pay given the priority of price stability. It is quite remarkable how the social commitment to avoid unnecessary unemployment has relatively dimmed as a political objective in contemporary Europe. Even in terms of availability and use of systematic information, there is much more focus on the facts of, and factors behind, inflationary possibilities (the Bank of England's *Inflation Report* is a good example) than on such matters as poverty and unemployment.[13] The priorities that have effectively emerged in official European policies not only bias what is done for the lives of people, but also what we systematically know about these lives.

It might be thought that what I am discussing here is the acceptability of the idea of a so-called 'natural rate of unemployment' to keep prices stable. The 'natural rate' is defined as that rate of unemployment below which the inflationary pressures would be dangerously strong. Many economists deny that such relationships exist in that form, claiming that much would depend on other policies and circumstances. Others have argued for the practical as well as scientific merit of thinking in terms of a natural rate of unemployment.[14]

This is certainly an important issue. But the disputes are not just about pure theory; they are also about actual numbers. Even in the perspective of presumed natural rates, Edmund Phelps—a distinguished economist who is a principal author of the concept of the 'natural rate'—has noted that 'no one would put Europe's natural rates at the double-digit levels exhibited by the unemployment rates in the past year', and that 'there is ample evidence that present unemployment rates exceed natural rates'.[15] So, no matter whether the idea of a natural rate of unemployment is accepted or not, it is hard to escape the diagnosis that what goes frequently for financial conservatism in Europe is more like radicalism with a systematic bias against giving priority to employment.

Costs of deficit and the balancing of priorities

Financial conservatism consists not only in a general inclination to attach importance to macroeconomic stability, including price stability, but also a willingness to be cautious in not opting for strategies that may be relatively costless now, but which might make it likely that the economy will take a plunge in the direction of more high-cost scenarios in the future (because of 'dynamic instability'). What we must distinguish from financial conservatism is 'anti-deficit radicalism' or 'anti-inflation radicalism', irrespective of the costs and benefits involved in that militancy.

It is, thus, necessary to take note of the rationale of financial conservatism *along with* giving adequate recognition to the social commitments of a contemporary society. In line with the rationale of financial conservatism, we must take note *both* of (1) the clearly identified costs of financial overstretching, *and* (2) the long-run risks of macroeconomic instability. The budgetary limits have to be reflected in the assessment of costs and benefits of giving priority to major social commitments. At the formal level of economic calculation, it is a question of taking note of the real 'cost' of deficit.[16] That cost, which is nothing other than the *scarcity value* of budgetary resources, would apply to the use of public resources of all kinds, and need not have a more adverse effect on major social commitments than it has on other public charges.

It is a price that has to be paid for drawing on scarce budgetary resources and would apply to *all* public spending varying from military expenditure and the deficit of loss-making public firms to public expenditures on health, education, poverty relief, and social insurance. The importance of social commitment for health care, basic education, the prevention of poverty, and social security will not be tarnished by the fact that funds for these crucial commitments have to compete with funds for other purposes (including military expenditure, and other preoccupations of many states, including the bearing of losses of ineffective public enterprises). In an economically scrutinized form, they can win even after taking note of the cost of funds, compared with other uses, which must also take note of the scarcity of public funds. Those who argue for a socially responsible vision of Europe have nothing much to gain from denying the importance of conservatism in financial balance. If social commitments are important—and many of them overwhelmingly are—they do not have to be supported by assuming or imagining that funds are *not* scarce. And some socially valuable objectives, particularly that of raising employment and cutting worklessness, would directly help in reducing public expenditure (in this case, to support the unemployed).

Social choice theory and public discussion

It is useful here to invoke the modelling of public decisions that is standard in social choice theory: a rather formal branch of contemporary economics and political theory. It is a discipline that originated in the systematic work done by French mathematicians in the eighteenth century, led by Condorcet and Borda, on social or group decisions. They were concerned with processes of election and the derivation of agreed decisions despite differences in preferences and interests. Over the last half century, quite an extensive technical literature has developed in this field.[17] The subject of public participation in social decisions belongs solidly to this field, and a number of technical results have clear bearing on what it is or is not possible to do in arriving at acceptable decisions despite differences in values and interests.[18]

It is not my purpose here to go into technical results, but only to point out that a general 'social-choice' approach is an important necessity in dealing with the social dilemmas we are concerned with in the contemporary world. What is needed is not some highly technical solution to our predicament, but agreed remedies that work, partly helped by the fact that they are agreed. Discussions and arguments contribute to the formation and revision of priorities and, as Frank Knight noted, 'values are established or validated and recognized through *discussion*, an activity which is at once social, intellectual, and creative'.[19] James Buchanan, whose 'public-choice' approach adds an important dimension to the analysis of social choice, is right to emphasize the fact that a democracy is 'government by discussion', and that 'individual values can and do change in the process of decision-making'.[20]

While professional economics has much to offer to explain and quantify the costs and benefits of alternative courses of action, the basic issues are very open to general public discussion. The idea of the 'cost' of public funds is not a hard one to grasp and to bring into the arena of public deliberation. Drawing on public resources involves costs both in the form of immediate sacrifices and in terms of risk of macroeconomic instability. We have to be cautious in demanding public funds for this or that. That qualification applies to *all* fields of public expenditure, each of which is open to public discussion, without exception: military expenditure, policing, the construction of prisons, and so on—not just the funds for helping the unemployed, the sick, the poor.

After accepting the need for caution and moderation, priorities still have to be drawn, and that calls for open discussion of all the competing claims on public funds. Public debates and exchanges can take all this into account and still be broad based and widely shared in discussing the relative priorities in using scarce funds. Indeed, this is one part of the basic social commitment—that of public participation in decision-taking—to which reference was made earlier.

Reform by consensus

How feasible is it to have responsible and peaceful public discussion on the need for balancing the conflicting demands of social commitment and financial conservatism? Much would depend here on the manner in which such discussion is proposed. The massive resistance to reform of social security in, say, France in the first few months of Chirac's government was not unconnected with the one-sided decision by the government to carry out unilateral pruning, with very little preceding discussion and negotiation. Reform by fiat that results from purely governmental decision, based on some technical arguments and not much consultation, can hardly be compared with a process of reform that emanates from public discussion of the necessity to go in that direction.

Michael Bruno, whom I have quoted earlier, and who was the architect of economic reform in Israel during 1985–86, has written an illuminating book on the experience of Israel in bringing about this change. The process of negotiation and the emergence of agreed policies were central to the success of the remarkable Israeli experience which saw the taming of a truly massive spiral of inflation. Bruno's book has an interesting title, namely *Crisis, Stabilization, and Economic Reform*, but an even more apt subtitle: *Therapy by Consensus*.[21] To question and re-examine the priorities of public policy is not a violation of social commitment, and may indeed be a necessity, but to try to force a solution without consultation and a search for consensus would certainly be an important violation, apart from probably being unfeasible in a functioning democracy.

European dilemmas

I discussed earlier the high levels of unemployment in Europe and the argument that they cannot be justified on grounds of economic stability and financial conservatism. The objectives of financial control seem to have stronger 'anti-inflation' features than any other commitment, including the objective of avoiding unnecessary unemployment. The anti-inflationary priorities cannot be justified, it appears, even on the basis of theories that argue for the importance of the so-called 'natural rate of unemployment'.

Underlying this situation is a more basic problem: that these priorities have been subjected to inadequate public discussion. That lacuna has a bearing both on the nature and characteristics of the criteria used and on their general acceptability and public endorsement.[22] I shall have to come back to this question.

To this 'anti-inflation radicalism' other priorities have been added in recent years that arise from the commitment to move rapidly to a common European currency. The criteria to be fulfilled for this monetary union, as laid down in Maastricht, requires that the ratio of general net borrowing should not exceed 3 per cent of the GDP and the government's gross debt should not be higher than 60 per cent of the GDP (or should, at least, approach that rate). In 1995 only Luxembourg fulfilled these requirements comfortably, with Germany hovering around meeting them. The commitment to get this situation reversed by the target date of 1999 has added another policy compulsion which many European economies will find hard to meet.

This challenge relates, of course, to the bigger question of the nature of the desired European unity. It is not difficult to see the force of arguments for greater integration of the European economies, which would ultimately include a common currency. There are many issues to sort out about what kind of an integrated Europe to have, and there are foundational questions too involving, as Tommaso Padoa-Schioppa notes, the contrast between 'Jean Monnet's functionalism and Altiero Spinelli's constitutionalism'.[23]

There are also questions about the speed at which this integration should be achieved, and whether exemptions may be made to the required conditions laid down at Maastricht.

In fact, the Maastricht agreement covered a wide agenda, including a social chapter as well as financial requirements. What is striking is not the narrowness of the format, but the extent to which public discussion has been dominated by one part of it, namely the financial conditionalities, to the relative neglect of the social concerns. It is not surprising that the central banks have gone in that direction; it is specifically their job to worry about the financial side of the economic picture. But the social priorities of reducing unemployment, diminishing poverty and emphasizing economic justice need more championing from the political movements in the respective countries. This is all the more important because the necessity of reducing budgetary deficits—not just for the sake of Maastricht but also for domestic economic stability—would require harsh steps to be taken, and the need for equity is never greater than when sacrifices have to be made. There is also great urgency in looking for innovative means for expanding employment and for making social services serve the neediest, rather than those who happen to be privileged, for one reason or another, in ongoing arrangements.

All this calls for much more public discussion and debate, rather than for sudden and precipitate action with little consultation. The unilateral policy decision by the French government in 1995 that led to turmoil on the streets of France, and had to be followed by equally unilateral eschewal of some of the major planks of the announced policy, did not make things easier, in the long run, for 'therapy by consensus' (to use Bruno's phrase). More discussion (with systematic use of information to outline the pros and cons) is needed not only in France but also in Britain (with a government basically hostile to a common currency) and even in Germany and Italy (with greater governmental support of the proposed programme, but many hard steps have yet to be taken).

The demands of European economic integration (including its monetary components) must be viewed in broader terms. Clearly, note must be taken of the real need that exists to bring down the size of budget deficits, quite irrespective of any plan of monetary integration. But the relation between cutting deficits, maintaining currency values and preventing inflation must be put in the context of other objectives, including the reduction of unemployment and of poverty in Europe. The central task is not just one of getting good professional answers to hard technical questions (important though it is) but also of arriving at decisions on a participatory basis, with adequate opportunity for people to air, and to press for, their concerns, including those about unemployment and hardship.

A more genuinely participatory process cannot but produce more emphasis on the importance of the unemployment problem and the associated deprivations. These problems call for more visionary proposals including ways in which the labour market can be influenced to expand employment and to raise take-home pay, and also what can be guaranteed for the least advantaged with efficiency and stability.[24] The recognition of unemployment reduction and the elimination of poverty as general *European priorities* would do much to remove the implicit bias in programmes dominated by monetary concerns.

If the programme of European unity looks today more and more like technical plans for unifying currencies and sticking to time-tables of budgetary cuts, it is important to be reminded that underlying that call for unity are bigger objectives that involve social commitment to the well-being and basic freedoms of the involved population. That commitment, on one side, includes giving priority to tackling deprivations which blight the lives of so many people at this time and, on the other side, also includes the practical freedom of the affected people to join in the process of decision-making, rather than simply being told what the experts think should now happen. Big issues concerning the process as well as the substance of policy decisions remain to be addressed.

Scrutiny of public expenditure and military spending

The need to scrutinize different types of public expenditure is strong in most countries in the world; the rich countries in Europe and North America as well as the poor economies in Africa, Asia and Latin America.[25] But the scrutiny has to be impartial, not only covering social security and welfare programmes but also other avenues of public expenditure. The fact that France was conducting nuclear tests at the time when the governmental proposals for cuts in public expenditures were announced did not help those proposals. The problem is, of course, a general one, and not special to France alone.

In his recent 'Anniversary Address' to the Royal Society, its retiring President, Sir Michael Atiyah, had the following to say on the British commitment to nuclear weapons in particular and military expenditures in general:

> I believe history will show that the insistence on a UK nuclear capability was fundamentally misguided, a total waste of resources and a significant factor in our relative economic decline over the past 50 years.
>
> The facts are easy to come by. Comparisons with Germany will show that both countries have devoted approximately the same fraction of their resources to Research and Development. However the division between civil and military R&D in the two countries is very different. Given this discrepancy, and the acknowledged importance of science and technology for modern industry, it would have required gross incompetence on the part of our German competitors if they had not derived a major economic benefit from this additional investment. Very similar remarks apply to Japan.[26]

What is most important to resist at this time is the placing of some parts of public policy beyond the domain of public debate, while keeping other parts firmly open to critical onslaught.

Social commitment and participatory choice

I should conclude this discussion with a few general remarks. First, the conflict between extensive social commitments and strong financial conservatism is a social dilemma precisely because there is much to be said for each. It is a question of balancing different good things, not one of opting for the 'good' against the 'bad'.

Second, social commitments arise from the recognition of the interdependence of the lives of different people in the society, leading to obligations towards each other that relate to the mutuality of their economic, political and social relations. This recognition is not new and goes back to the philosophical writings of such authors as Immanuel Kant and Adam Smith.

Third, while 'the spirit of capitalism' is often seen as being hostile to the commitments of the state and of the civil society, in fact the growth of capitalism has done much to strengthen these commitments, both through increased interdependence and through enhanced prosperity. More dialectically, the recognition that increased prosperity of some can go with continued deprivation of others has also strengthened the argument for special commitment to those who are less favoured by the economic process. The socialist critique, which links with disparities in capitalism, remains relevant today, even though the particular socialist remedies have been much undermined by practical failures. The importance of looking for fresh institutional answers cannot be overstated, but the need for dealing with inequalities and deprivation remains as strong as ever.

Fourth, the nature of the obligations of the society can be formulated under the general heading of 'individual freedom as a social commitment'. The social commitments include not only provisions such as health care, basic education, poverty alleviation and social security (without which the exercise of individual freedom would be most restricted) but also elementary liberties and political and civil rights, including the right to participate in public decisions affecting the lives of people. Participatory opportunity is one of the basic social commitments that is central to addressing the social dilemmas we face today.

Fifth, the case for financial conservatism is strong, and that strength relates both to the immediate economic harms of over-spending, and also to the risk of escalation and the danger of dynamic instability. But the case for financial conservatism has to be distinguished from the advocacy for what are in effect 'balanced-budget radicalism' and 'anti-inflation radicalism'. Those 'extremist' solutions can extract heavy penalties in terms of economic insecurity for the deprived and underprivileged (and also through unnecessarily high unemployment), as well as public unrest associated with the execution of unnegotiated radicalism without any consensus.

Sixth, the exercise of balanced-budget radicalism in the United States is not only causing impasse in its governance but will also force more sacrifices on the part of the relatively deprived than is needed for the sound objectives of financial conservatism. The demand for complete elimination of a budget deficit within just a few years is not based on a pragmatic reading of the nature and state of the US economy. The social costs of the proposed withdrawals have to be compared with the economic benefits of lower, or zero, budget deficit, and also with the social role of other public expenditures (such as military spending as well as subsidies to the relatively rich under diverse support programmes).

Seventh, these social dilemmas are strong in Europe particularly because of the priority that inflation control has tended to receive over the removal of unemployment. The need for budgetary discipline has now been reinforced by the demands of the programme for a monetary union. Those demands have been used to justify unilateral attempts by governments to cut many of the existing programmes (with little success and much turmoil in France), but the entire process calls for a more democratic solution (based on more widespread and informed discussion and greater opportunity for airing concerns and for suggesting imaginative reforms). A more participatory process would not only make 'therapy by consensus' easier, it might also help to remove the relative neglect of unemployment and poverty *vis-à-vis* other objectives. The demands of 'individual freedom as a social commitment' include participation in decisions that are crucial to the lives of the people involved.*

Eighth, in addition to giving fuller recognition to the role of public debates, it is crucial to broaden the scope and content of these discussions. The agenda has often been set by one group of worries (legitimate on their own, but none the less deeply incomplete in coverage), while some of the economic debates on financial discipline have tended to look rather alienated from the concerns of the people. A clearer examination of the need for a common European commitment to the maintenance of a high level of employment and to the eradication of poverty would make a major difference to the nature of the debates, which have tended to concentrate too exclusively on disciplining budget deficits and controlling the dangers of inflation. The strengthening of public participation and the broadening of the coverage of public debates are complementary objectives and can reinforce one another.

Ninth, it is important not only to distinguish between financial conservatism and anti-deficit radicalism, but also to re-examine all the claims on public funds—from the military to the civil and the social—in conducting public discussions and debates. Many fields of public expenditure in Europe as well as North America have escaped substantial critical scrutiny, including the balancing of priorities in military *vis-à-vis* civil programmes. The comparative assessments that are needed involve not only the arrangements for health care, social security and pensions but also the priorities of long-run research on which the future well-being of the citizens crucially depend. These commitments have to be compared with the allocations for military and other expenditure, including research and development for military purposes. The rationale of financial conservatism requires that critical examination has to be

---

* In many ways, this takes us back exactly to the issues that, in the final years of the Second World War, engaged the attention of democratic and egalitarian political theorists and leaders such as Eugenio Colorni and Altiero Spinelli.

quite general, with no hallowed exemptions. The quality of scrutiny is not strained.

Finally, the social dilemmas can be solved only through processes of participatory social choice, including open dialogues and debates. The stakes include the ultimate ends, but also the practical means, and, most importantly, the procedures through which these ends and means are assessed. Unilateral guidance, even by the very best of experts, does not, in itself, offer a solution.

Do Liberty and Equality Conflict?

RONALD DWORKIN

How shall we decide?

It is now a staple of conservative political rhetoric that the two great Enlightenment virtues, liberty and equality, are not allies but enemies, and that people who love liberty must therefore despise any egalitarian project. Conservatives denounce standard measures used to decrease inequality and poverty, like redistributive taxation and minimum wage laws, as tyranny. Taxation is particularly odious, they say, because it takes people's property by force, and uses it in ways they have not chosen and may not approve. The same assumption—that equality and liberty conflict as ideals—is equally prominent on the left of politics. People who describe themselves as egalitarians insist that a 'bourgeois' concern for liberty has frustrated their goal; they declare that many of the opportunities people of means now have—to private education or medicine, for example—should be taken from them. Some feminists and anti-racists argue that a commitment to liberties like freedom of speech has crippled progress toward gender and racial equality: they insist that many forms of sexually explicit or racist expression should be banned. The idea that liberty and equality conflict has also exercised great influence in the nascent democracies of Eastern Europe. Many politicians, activists, and students there declare that genuine liberty can be obtained only by rejecting the goals of economic equality altogether: they point to the Communists who until recently tyrannized them in equality's name. It is a matter of more than only academic philosophical concern, then, whether the popular assumption that a society must choose between the two great ideals is correct.

Of course some political values or ideals do conflict with one another, in the sense that a policy that serves one often compromises the other. Liberty sometimes conflicts with security, for example: a community may be forced to choose between banning an unpopular political group and running an increased risk of violent injury to individuals. Does equality also conflict with liberty in some similar way, so that we must sometimes give up one to protect the other? There is no doubt that the terms 'liberty' and 'equality' can be defined in such a way that, so defined, they do indeed conflict, steadily and relentlessly. Suppose we define equality, for example, as the situation in which everyone in a given political community has the same wealth, no matter how much each has consumed, how hard each has worked or at what enterprise. Suppose we then define liberty as the situation in which government prevents no one from doing anything at all he or she wishes, and takes no share of anyone's gross income as taxation. Then of course equality and liberty would conflict.

These are hopeless accounts of liberty and equality, for a reason I must now explain. 'Liberty' and 'equality' name abstract political ideals, which must be interpreted before they can be applied to concrete political issues. Politicians and citizens disagree about whether taxation is an invasion of liberty, or whether reverse discrimination offends equality, not because they speak different languages, but because they are drawn to different and competing interpretations of the two ideals. They have different understandings of how best to define or express the more fundamental values that the political ideals embody or protect. We must judge any theory of liberty or of equality in that light. We must ask whether it is a *successful* interpretation, that is, whether it succeeds in expressing what is *good* about the ideal it purports to explain.

That is particularly important in the present context. The proposition that some of our political ideals conflict with others is significant and threatening, because, if it is true, a community must have cause for moral regret in some circumstances no matter what it does. It must choose between two evils. We cannot sustain that claim unless we have defined the ideals in question to show that something of genuine value is lost, or some important principle dishonoured, whenever the ideal is set aside.

The crude theories of liberty and equality that I just mentioned, according to which they plainly do conflict, fail this interpretative test, because they do not express any values at all. On the contrary, they convert what are supposed to be political virtues into vices. It is obviously wrong that people should have the same wealth no matter how hard some have worked and saved while others rested and consumed. It is obviously wrong that some people should be free to murder or steal from others. Our objection to these states of affairs is not that though they are desirable in themselves they conflict with other values we want to promote. It is rather that they are bad in themselves. We sacrifice nothing of value by not rewarding the purposefully idle or by thwarting the murderous. So we must reject these interpretations and search for other, better ones, before we can decide whether, on the *best* interpretations of liberty and equality, the conservatives are right that minimum-wage laws and high taxes invade liberty or the radicals are right who say that freedom of speech is an obstacle to equality.

It might be said, in reply, that my argument has begun in the wrong direction. We should aim to find, not a rose-coloured interpretation of liberty and equality that shows each to its best advantage, but rather the most accurate interpretation, one that shows the ideals as they really are. That advice makes no sense, because we are hoping better to understand not a phenomenon of nature, like a comet, whose character is independent of any value it might have for human beings, but abstract ideals whose 'true' nature, as I just said, cannot be identified *except* through an interpretative process that tries to find, in the traditions in which these ideals figure, more fundamental principles or values they can be taken to exemplify. Only then can we intelligently decide more concrete questions of application—whether affirmative action programmes violate equality, for example—by asking which answer better serves that understanding of the ideal's point.[1] Of course, our interpretations must in the end make sense to us; they must not depart too far from our previous paradigms. We could not accept any interpretation of equality, no matter how otherwise compelling, if it declared slavery to be an egalitarian institution. We could not accept any account of liberty that declared a community of forced labour a free society. But these firm paradigms leave room for many different interpretations of both ideals, and we must fix on one for each value that we think provides its best grounding in more fundamental values. Only then can we decide more controversial questions about whether some act offends the ideal, or whether, so interpreted, the two ideals conflict.

Ethical individualism

We must begin, therefore, at a relatively basic level. We must try to identify more fundamental values that the political ideals of liberty and equality, as they have figured in our political traditions, might be understood to exemplify. I propose that we start with two more fundamental principles that are very widely accepted in contemporary humanist societies: together they make up a general moral outlook that I shall call ethical individualism. If we can find an interpretation of liberty and equality that shows that these ideals respect and enforce the two principles of ethical individualism, we will have succeeded in showing what is good about them.

The first of these principles is the principle of equal value. It holds that it is intrinsically, objectively, and equally important that human beings lead successful lives; important that once any human life has begun it flourishes rather than founders, and, above all, that it not be wasted. That does not mean that all human beings are in fact equally good, or equally worthy of respect or admiration, or that all human lives are in fact equally successful or valuable for their agents or for others. It insists only that it is equally important, from an objective point of view, that all human lives flourish.

Most of us already accept that principle. You think it is important what you do with your own life, not just because you happen to want to make something of it, but because you *should* want to make something of it. You think that, if for some reason you ceased to care how your life went, you would be making a mistake. If so, you believe it is objectively important how you live. Is there anything different about you that could make that true for your life but not everyone's? You might toy with a positive answer. Yes, it is because I am a member of God's chosen people. Or because I have been given a great talent that must not be wasted. There is nothing logically wrong with these answers, nothing that shows them to be irrational. But that is not what you think, at least on reflection. We know we are different from one another. We have different backgrounds, traditions and talents, and each of us should live in a way that is appropriate to who and what he is. But these personal qualities are part of the challenge we face in living well, not reasons why we face that challenge. We do not think that it would not matter how we lived if we were not Jews or muscular or French or poets. We think it is important how we live for no more concrete reason than that we have a life to lead, because we are humans and mortal.

The second principle of ethical individualism—the principle of special responsibility—declares that the connection between you and your life is nevertheless a special one. Someone who treated his own life as having no different place in his plans and no greater call on his attention than the life of any stranger would be not a saint but a Martian. The second principle insists that this special relationship is best understood as one of special responsibility, that living is an assignment we can execute well or badly. The assignment includes an intellectual challenge: to live out of a conception of what makes a life successful that is personal, in the sense that the agent has embraced it, rather than political in the sense that it has been thrust upon him. Living well, on this view, requires both personal commitment and a social environment in which that commitment is encouraged and respected.

I shall try to defend interpretations of equality and liberty that are rooted in these two principles of ethical individualism. But since the first principle seems more egalitarian in content than the second, and the second seems more related to liberty, it is worth emphasizing that the two premisses do not conflict in themselves. The first—of equal value—does not contradict the second because it does not require that I accept responsibility for the success of any life but my own; it requires only that I acknowledge that from an impersonal point of view—the view appropriate to the government of a political community, for example—my own fate should matter no more than any one else's.

Equality

Any government that accepts the first principle of ethical individualism must display at least motivational equality toward its own citizens: it must treat them all with equal concern.* But equality, as a political virtue, demands more than this. It demands, not just an attitude, but concrete institutions. So our account of equality must go further: it must describe the state of affairs at which a society should aim if it accepts that motivational equality means economic equality as well.

We face an important threshold question. Should such a society aim to make people equal in their welfare, that is, equal in their pleasure, or happiness, or satisfaction, or achievement, or well-being defined in some other way? Or should it aim to make them equal in the resources they control? The difference is crucial one.[2] Equality of welfare is a deeply unattractive (and, anyway, scarcely intelli-

---

* That requirement can be accepted even by people who reject any form of equality as a political goal. Utilitarianism (which is particularly popular, just now, with political conservatives) argues that a community's resources should be distributed not equally, but so as to maximize the welfare or well-being of citizens on *average*. That means refusing to adopt welfare programmes that will help those at the bottom but only by taking money in taxes from the majority and so lowering the average welfare of the community as a whole. Utilitarianism is said by its proponents to respect motivational equality because it counts gains or losses to everyone, including those at the bottom, in the same way in determining which structures and decisions do improve well-being on average. That seems an inadequate way to treat people with equal concern, but I shall not pursue the point here.

gible) ideal for a variety of reasons, one of which it is important to emphasize now. Any community that actually attempted to make people equal in well-being would need a *collective* identification of what well-being is—of what makes one life better or more success-ful than another—and any collective identification would violate both the principles of ethical individualism. Since different people have very different ambitions and ideals for their lives, a community that based its entire system of production and distribution on a single, collective answer—for example, that a successful life is one with as much pleasure as possible—would hardly treat everyone with equal concern. And it would, in any case, violate the principle of special responsibility, which reserves that decision to individuals. So any conception of equality that respects ethical individualism must aim to make people equal, not in well-being judged from some collective point of view, but in the resources each controls. In a society that is egalitarian in that sense, people are free to decide how to use their equal share of resources to achieve higher well-being or a better life as *they* judge that, each for himself or herself. Equality of resources, in other words, is a liberal conception of equality.

What is an equal share of resources?[3] Critics of equality often assume that it means that everyone should have *identical* resources, quite independently of what each chooses to do or be; that people must have the same bank-account balance, for example, even though one chooses to work longer or harder than the other. I said earlier that any interpretation of equality that has that consequence must fail. On any attractive conception, those who choose to be idle, or to write philosophy rather than produce what others value more highly and so would pay more to acquire, should have less income for that reason. Those choices might be right for them, in the exercise of their responsibility for their own lives. But true equality requires that such choices be made with an eye to their conse-quences for others, and that people's resources should therefore be sensitive to the choices they make.

So we need a different model. I suggest this one: a fully equal dis-tribution of resources is one in which no one 'envies' the resources others have. Envy, in this context, is an economic, not psychological, phenomenon. Someone envies the resources of another when he would prefer those resources, and the pattern of work and consumption that produces them, to his own resources and choices. This envy test may be met even when people's welfare or well-being is not equal. If your goals or ambitions or projects are more easily satisfied than mine, or if your personality is otherwise different in some pertinent way, you may achieve a higher level of well-being, at least in your own eyes, than I do from the same resources. Equality of resources is very different from equality of welfare.

I can illustrate this liberal conception of equality through an imaginary story. Suppose a group of people is shipwrecked on an island with abundant resources of many different kinds. How could they distribute these resources equally? Under a certain assumption, which I shall describe in a moment, the envy test would be met, and perfect distributional equality secured, if all the resources were auctioned, and everyone on the island had an equal number of auction tokens to bid with. If such an auction were repeated until no one wished it to be run again, and it did finally stop, the envy test would be met. No one would prefer the bundle of resources anyone else secured in the auction; if he had preferred another's bundle, he would have acquired that bundle in place of his own. Once the auction was complete, people would be free to manufacture, labour, trade, invest and consume as they wished from the initial envy-free stock of resources. Since each would anticipate this in deciding what resources to bid to acquire, the distribution of resources and wealth would continue to be equal, even though each person's holdings would be different.

But that is true only under the assumption that the bidders in the auction are equal in other respects. The resources people control are of two kinds: personal and impersonal. Personal resources are physical and mental capacities of different kinds, including health and talent, that affect people's success in achieving their plans and projects. Impersonal resources are parts of the environment that can be owned and transferred, like money, land, raw materials, houses, and computers, and various legal rights and interests in these kinds of resources. The auction I just imagined is an auction of impersonal resources, and if personal resources are and remain unequal, the envy test will not be satisfied, either during or after the auction. Even if my impersonal resources are the same as yours, I will envy your total set of resources, which includes your talent and health as well. Once the auction has stopped, moreover, and people begin to produce and trade, your advantages in talent and health will soon destroy our initial equality in impersonal resources as well. So will differences in the luck we have. Your life may prosper and mine decline because of my brute bad luck; my bad luck, I mean, with respect to risks I could not have anticipated and did not choose to run.

If we tried to model an egalitarian economy in the real world on this imaginary story, therefore, we could not simply distribute resources equally, as in the auction, and then accept whatever distribution production and trade produced from that initial situation. We would have to introduce compensatory strategies to repair, so far as this can be done, inequalities in personal capabilities and in brute luck. We cannot compensate for these inequalities perfectly, however, and schemes with the most obvious initial egalitarian appeal would in fact fail. Suppose a community, anxious to restore an initial resource equality, simply transferred wealth from the rich to the poor once a year until the envy test over impersonal resources was met once again. That policy would obviously affect what goods people decided to produce and what services they decided to offer, to the disadvantage of some other people, including some of those the redistribution was designed to help. They might find that they could not buy, even with their improved wealth, what they could before because this was no longer produced or available.[4] It does not follow that no compensatory scheme that affects production or price can be justified. It rather means that any such scheme must be justified in a particular way—by showing those who lose by it that it nevertheless unambiguously improves equality of resources. That is a highly theoretical statement of a practical problem that any democratic politician faces who wishes to improve equality. He or she must find arguments that explain why some particular form of redistribution of wealth is required by fairness, up to a particular point, though not permitted beyond it.

At least one compensatory strategy can be defended in that way. Return, for the moment, to the desert island. Suppose we had added, to the resources available at auction, insurance policies offering protection against a variety of risks including accident, sickness and low income, in return for premiums that the auction would fix, subject only to the stipulation that premiums for any particular coverage be based on average rather than individual actuarial risk. To the extent people chose to purchase such policies in the auction, sacrificing other resources to do so, the post-auction situation would produce less envy.

In real world situations, we can devise a system of taxation and redistribution, either in funds, in opportunities for employment or in resources like medical care, which is modelled on that hypothetical insurance market. We can ask what insurance people with equal resources, and with the knowledge and attitudes most people in our community actually have, would have purchased on those terms. That question cannot be answered with any precision, but we can nevertheless use rough or approximate answers to design a progressive tax system: the aggregate taxes levied in that design would equal the premiums that it is plausible to assume would have been paid, and redistribution to the sick, unemployed and poor would equal the total insurance coverage those premiums would have bought.[5] This redistributive taxation would not wholly compensate—the envy test would not be fully met even if such a programme were in place—but it would unproblematically reduce inequality in resources. No one who accepts the basic principles of liberal equality could consistently reject redistribution at least to that level.[6]

Liberty

The second principle of ethical individualism is particularly pertinent to liberty, and it might be thought to provide, on its own, a sufficient explanation of what more fundamental value that political virtue is best understood as protecting. People have a special responsibility to design their lives for themselves, so far as they are able to do so, in response to their own convictions about the character of a good life. Liberty protects that responsibility because, when a government invades liberty, it diminishes people's range of opportunities and choices, leaving them with less power to bend their lives to their own values.

But the breadth of that initial intuition raises an immediate problem, because only certain ways in which government reduces opportunity have been thought to raise issues of liberty. This distinction is captured in the very popular interpretation of political liberty that, following Isaiah Berlin's well-known distinction, I shall call the 'negative-liberty' conception.[7] According to that conception, someone's liberty is his power to do what he might want, and otherwise be able to do, free from prohibition by government. My present liberty would be decreased by a law establishing a new one-way traffic system, therefore, but not by a law cutting my welfare benefits so that I can no longer afford to drive at all. But of course my range of choice—the set of opportunities actually open to me— is more sharply restricted by the second law than by the first. If liberty is a value because it protects opportunity, why should we accept any interpretation of it that distinguishes between the two laws in that way?

It will not do simply to declare that liberty, properly understood, just *is* compromised by the former law but not by the latter. Liberty is an abstract and contested concept, and we identify and defend conceptions of it only through the normative interpretation I described. Can we defend the idea captured in the negative-liberty conception—that liberty is compromised by official prohibitions but not by other official acts that also decrease opportunity—by showing that liberty protects a special value when it is defined in that way?

Here are three suggestions. We might argue, first, that the opportunities threatened by official prohibitions are in some way more central or fundamental or important than those that government curtails in other ways. Or, second, that prohibitions are particularly offensive ways of curtailing opportunities because it is in principle wrong for government to dictate to people how to live. Or, third, that it is important to distinguish between laws that assign property-interests to people (including social-benefit laws as well as inheritance laws and other rules of ownership) and those that stipulate what people may do with the property so assigned (including traffic regulations and the more serious parts of the criminal and tort law). Each of these three suggestions is of the right form, because each purports to identify some reason for treating prohibitions differently from other official acts. Each is, in fact, a helpful suggestion, though (as we shall now see) pursuing them supports not the negative-liberty conception, but a very different, more limited ideal that I shall call the liberal conception of liberty.

Consider the first suggestion: that the opportunities government denies by prohibitions are more fundamental or important than those it affects in other ways. That is plainly not true in general: some financial decisions, including altering welfare benefits, destroy many more important opportunities than some prohibitions, such as traffic regulations, do. It is, nevertheless, true that governments have used criminal prohibitions and injunctions to deprive citizens of opportunities that are indeed fundamental ones: the opportunities of free speech, and freedom of conscience and religion, for example. We might describe these as *basic* liberties, and insist that a political ideal of liberty should be defined so as to give those basic liberties a prominent place and special legal protection, as they are given, for example, under the United States Constitution, which invalidates any law infringing them.

The second suggestion—that prohibitions are particularly offensive forms of political action—is also plainly false as a general proposition. There is nothing insulting in forbidding murder and assault. But some forms of prohibition are indeed offensive for a special reason, which we can identify if we distinguish between two kinds of justification a government might have for some official act that deprives citizens of opportunities. (This distinction is not intended to be exhaustive.) The first argues that the constraint is necessary to protect the opportunities or interests of other people. Government has that justification for laws against murder. The second argues that the constraint is needed to force people to lead better, more appropriate lives. Some societies (including our own) have offered that justification for laws requiring religious observance in a certain faith, or criminalizing homosexuality and contraception, for example. Political acts of the second kind are inherently damaging to the principle of individual responsibility that liberty, on our account, is meant to protect, and such acts typically, though not invariably, take the form of criminal prohibitions. (Savage taxes on conduct deemed immoral—on gambling, for example—are exceptions.) So we should define the political value of liberty to include the idea that certain kinds of prohibition are in themselves offensive to liberty; moralizing prohibitions that can only be defended as attempts to impose on individual citizens some collective view of what kinds of life are worthy.

The last suggestion—that there is a morally important difference between laws that assign property and those that limit the use of property that has been assigned—seems right in principle. A community that wished to leave its citizens the maximum range of opportunity to live as they thought appropriate would be required, just for that reason, to distribute and protect property of different sort. I cannot design a life for myself unless I know what resources I may use in living it, and unless I am secure in my control of those resources. But such a community would certainly have a general, standing reason not to limit how citizens may use the resources its scheme of property assigned to them. So we must add, to the liberal conception of liberty we are now constructing, a principle reflecting that distinction.

But now we face an important choice. Should that principle declare it to be an invasion of liberty whenever government constrains the use of property an individual actually controls? Or should it exempt constraints whose purpose is to *change* the scheme of property in force, on the ground that the control he exercises is not rightful? We can see the difference by considering an example. Suppose that I use old, polluting technology in my factory the effect of which is to lower the value of your neighbouring house. I and my customers save money, because I can produce and sell at a lower cost than if I modernized. This seems unfair, however, because you are bearing part of the true costs of my production. If the market were more efficient—if what economists call the 'externality' problem was resolved—my customers and I would bear those costs rather than you. In these circumstances, a law that prohibits me from using such equipment, unless I compensate you and others affected, might easily be defended as re-adjusting the distribution of property to make it fairer, as judged by the community's own standards of fairness.

Under the first version of the principle I proposed, which counts any constraint on the use of property as a loss in liberty, this law would indeed infringe my liberty, although justifiably so. But if we include this first version in our conception of liberty, we would violate the injunction I described earlier: that a successful interpretation of an attractive political ideal must show that a moral cost is incurred—that there is something for the community morally to regret—whenever that ideal is compromised. Surely there is nothing to regret in forcing me to compensate you for losses that I, not you, should have incurred, and a community faces no genuine conflict of any kind in deciding to do so. That suggests that we should make the second choice, and call invasions of liberty only those constraints that cannot be justified as enforcing the community's conception of rightful property.

But there is an overwhelming disadvantage to that choice, too. If we define liberty so that no constraint a government imposes in order to redistribute property can count as an infringement, we create an enormous loophole that calls our whole interpretation into question. I said, earlier, that we must reject out of hand any interpretation of liberty according to which massive constraints on freedom of employment or trade would not be regarded as deprivations of liberty. But the second version of our principle has exactly that consequence: a government imposing these draconian constraints could avoid any charge of compromising liberty by claiming, no doubt sincerely, that these constraints were needed to redistribute wealth in a way its conception of fairness required. It could make that claim, for example, if it embraced equality under one of the interpretations we have rejected—identical resources, for example, or equality of welfare—because equality so understood could only be achieved through the most domineering government imaginable, whose officials relentlessly controlled prices, investment, employment and consumption.

Conflict?

We can resolve this dilemma in only one way. We must choose a *third* version of the principle we are considering, according to which prohibitions or constraints are compromises of liberty only if they limit the use of property, or other resources in the hands of their *rightful* owner, not according to the community's own theory of just distribution, whatever it is, but according to the *best* or *soundest* such theory. So the draconian regulations would indeed compromise liberty because they are *not* required by justice. But it is important to notice that this is a solution to our dilemma only because we have settled on a theory of justice—equality of resources—that would not require or justify the centralist government I just described. Our interpretation of liberty, in other words, has now begun to depend on our prior interpretation of equality. We should not be surprised at this, because the two principles of ethical individualism we have been drawing on are part of the same overall ethical attitude, and so must be understood in the light of one another. Nevertheless, building our theory of equality into our interpretation of liberty might be thought grounds for an objection to the argument as a whole, and I shall have to consider that objection later.

In any case, the liberal conception of equality we defined does allow us to escape the dilemma, by adopting the third version of our principle, without producing a counter-intuitive account of liberty. Equality of resources does not require a *dirigiste* or socialist economy; on the contrary it cannot be achieved in such a society. It requires essentially a free market in capital, labour and consumption, and it intervenes in such markets not to replace but only to perfect them, either by correcting market imperfections of the kind economists standardly recognize, or by correcting a different kind of imperfection: the failure of actual markets to offer standard forms of insurance on terms that make it equally available to everyone. When it intervenes for the latter reason, moreover, it does so by taxing and redistributing the consequences of market transactions rather than by dictating transactions directly, as socialist economies do, and though, of course, taxation affects choice by affecting prices, it does so according to principles of fairness, reflecting assumptions about rightful ownership rather than economic dogma. The imaginary auction I described, to illustrate an ideal equality of resources, would be corrupted and wholly fail to achieve its goals if some official dictated how citizens were to bid, or the choices they were to make about investment, labour, consumption and insurance after the auction was over.

Nor would a government that sought equality of resources have to contravene either of the first two principles of the liberal conception of liberty. The first principle identifies fundamental liberties that are essential to a citizen's capacity to decide issues of fundamental personal and political value for himself, and the whole point of equality of resources, which is to allow individuals to make such decisions from an equal stock of wealth, depends on that capacity. The second principle requires moral independence from government, and the point of equality would also be destroyed without such independence. So, if equality of resources is our ideal of economic justice, we can accept the liberal conception of liberty we have now constructed with no compunction or sense of conflict at all.

We should test that happy conclusion by asking whether its implications for the concrete cases I mentioned at various points seem sound. Do minimum-wage laws, or laws censoring racial speech, abolishing private education, or imposing redistributive income or wealth taxes, advance equality of resources? Would they violate liberty on the liberal conception? When the answer to the first question is yes, the answer to the second is no, and vice versa. Some constraints that have been urged on egalitarian grounds—

flat prohibitions of private education, for example—violate fundamental rights necessary to the individual responsibility of parents
for their children. They are, therefore, violations of liberty. But they
are also, even in a very unequal society, violations of equality as well.
That follows from the fact that, even if wealth were distributed in
the way liberal equality requires, some citizens would want, and
would have the power to choose, a special (perhaps religious)
education for their children. Equality cannot be advanced by
putting any citizen in a worse position than he would enjoy if full,
genuine equality had been achieved.[8] We should take the same view
about censoring racial, sexist or pornographic speech. That is a
violation of liberty on the liberal conception, and, since it denies
some people an equal role in the formation of the community's
moral environment, it is a violation of equality as well.[9]

Other constraints, including minimum-wage laws, are different
in the crucial respect that they deny no one opportunities he would
have in a truly equal society. In such a community, no one would be
forced to sell his labour cheaply in order to live, and employers
would not have the opportunities of exploitation they now do.
So minimum-wage laws in our unjust society (at least if they have
the consequences their proponents predict) are not inegalitarian,
because they genuinely bring citizens closer to the positions they
would occupy if resources were equally divided. But exactly because
they are properly seen in that light, they are not invasions of liberty,
on the liberal conception, either. They must be classified as
strategies of justified redistribution rather than as constraints on
the use of rightful property.

What about taxation? I said, at the start, that conservatives denounce high progressive taxation as the paradigm case of violating
liberty to serve equality. It is certainly true that equality of resources
would justify much higher and more redistributive taxes than either
Britain or the United States, for example, now collects from its more
affluent citizens. But the claim that taxation compromises liberty is
particularly puzzling in many ways. Whatever plausibility it has
depends on the popular idea that taxation takes a taxpayer's money
away from him and gives it to others without his consent. But that
popular idea is doubly confused.

First, money taken in taxes is not 'owned' by the taxpayer before it is taken. Under some devices used for collection, it is true, he is allowed to retain it, temporarily, as a kind of trustee, and under other methods it is nominally included in his overall wages for certain accounting purposes. Neither of these devices is necessary. All income tax might be collected, after all, by a different arrangement under which people bargain for post-tax wages, and the tax is levied on employers as a proportion of their payroll, calculated, at progressive rates, employee by employee. That would neither forbid nor require taxpayers to do anything, nor would it deprive them of any funds that were even temporarily under their control or listed in a box on their wage statements. It would still be true, even then, that taxation would reduce the opportunity set of wealthy taxpayers: they could not buy what they could if payroll taxes were lower, because their wages would then be higher. But even on the negative-liberty conception, that does not count as a compromise or limitation on their liberty, any more than, on that conception, refusing to increase welfare benefits for the poor counts as limiting their liberty either.

Even if money taken in taxes were properly treated as taxpayers' money first, redistributive taxation, modelled on the hypothetical insurance exercise I described, or on some other strategy that unambiguously improves equality of resources, would still not invade liberty because it would be justified as seeking, rather than constraining, a rightful distribution of property. That is even more evident in the case of taxation than of minimum-wage laws, because it is even clearer that redistributive taxation that improves equality deprives no one of any opportunity he would have if equality were actually realized.

Did I rig the argument?

So we have answered our initial question. Liberty and equality, properly understood as protecting the principles of ethical individualism, are not conflicting ideals. Some critics may say, however, that the argument through which I reached that conclusion is a sham because (as they might put it) I begged the question by simply *defining* each virtue so that it would not conflict with the other. My argument did show, it is true, that we cannot interpret the great Enlightenment virtues of liberty and equality (or, I would add, community) in isolation from one another. We must interpret each, so far as possible, in the light of what we think about the other. We saw that, most dramatically, when we were trying to decide among alternate formulations of the third principle of liberty. We found that we could not avoid bringing the idea of distributive justice, and hence of equality, into the very formulation of what liberty means.

The charge of circularity or rigging is misplaced, however. Any competent interpretation of a political ideal must aim, as I said, to show why dishonouring it, even when this is justifiable, is always an occasion for moral regret. If we accept that requirement, then we cannot avoid asking, just in the process of interpreting liberty, whether measures like minimum-wage laws or redistributive taxes are such occasions, and we may find, on reflection, that this depends on whether such measures are just. We could avoid merging our interpretations of equality and liberty in that way only by abandoning the interpretative project altogether, and simply stipulating some 'descriptive' account of liberty like the negative-liberty conception. But there is no gain in clarity or in anything else—quite the contrary—in insisting on a definition that neither tracks the way an ideal figures in real politics nor shows us what is good about it. If that kind of stipulation really is necessary to produce a conflict between the two ideals, the conflict is a toothless one.

So we have come, by different routes, beginning in different traditions and paradigms, to conceptions of liberty and equality that seem not only compatible but mutually necessary. The two political virtues are only different aspects of the same fundamental humanist attitude—ethical individualism—that we began by inspecting, and which we now see to lie at the heart of liberalism itself.

Two Hundred Years of Reactionary Rhetoric: The Futility Thesis

ALBERT O. HIRSCHMAN

My starting point is the famous 1949 set of lectures by the English sociologist T. H. Marshall on the 'development of citizenship' in the West.[1] Marshall distinguished between the civil, political, and social dimensions of citizenship and then proceeded to explain, very much in the spirit of the Whig interpretation of history, how the more enlightened human societies had tackled one of these dimensions after the other, conveniently allocating about one century to each of the three tasks. According to this scheme, the eighteenth century witnessed the major battles for the institution of *civil* citizenship: from freedom of speech, thought, and religion to the right to even-handed justice and other aspects of individual freedom or, roughly, the 'Rights of Men' of the natural-law doctrine and of the American and French Revolutions. In the course of the nineteenth century, it was the *political* aspect of citizenship, that is, the right of citizens to participate in the exercise of political power, that made major strides as the right to vote was extended to ever larger groups. Finally, the rise of the welfare state in the twentieth century extended the concept of citizenship to the *social and economic* sphere, by recognizing that minimal conditions of education, health, economic well-being, and security are basic to the life of a civilized being as well as to the meaningful exercise of the civil and political attributes of citizenship.

My interest is in the hostile reactions that have followed upon

Marshall's three progressive waves. That interest was aroused by the sustained attack on the idea of the welfare state that we have witnessed recently. But, so I asked myself, is it not true that not just the last but each and every one of the three forward thrusts have been followed by ideological counter-thrusts of extraordinary force? The backlash so far experienced by the welfare state may, in fact, be rather mild in comparison with the earlier onslaughts and conflicts that followed upon the assertion of individual freedoms in the eighteenth century or upon the broadening of political participation in the nineteenth. Once we contemplate this protracted and perilous seesawing of action and reaction we come to appreciate more than ever the profound wisdom of Whitehead's well-known observation: '[T]he major advances in civilization are processes which all but wreck the societies in which they occur.'[2] It is surely this statement rather than any account of smooth, unrelenting progress that catches the deeply ambivalent essence of the story so blandly entitled the 'development of citizenship'.

Three reactions

There are good reasons, then, for focusing on the *reactions* to the successive forward thrusts. Let me briefly state what I understand by the 'three reactions', or reactionary waves.

The first reaction is the movement of ideas following (and opposing) the assertion of equality before the law and of civil rights in general: Marshall's civil component of citizenship. There is a major difficulty in isolating this movement. The most resounding assertion of these rights occurred in the early stages and as a result of the French Revolution so that the contemporary reaction against them was intertwined with opposition to the Revolution and all its works. Hence the radical counter-revolutionary discourse that soon emerged refused to distinguish between positive and negative aspects of the French Revolution or to concede that there were any positive ones. Anticipating what was later to become a slogan of the

Left ('la Révolution est un bloc'), the early adversaries of the Revolution considered it as a cohesive whole. Significantly, the first general indictment of the Revolution, Burke's *Reflections on the Revolution in France* (1790), started with a sustained polemic against the Declaration of the Rights of Man. Taking the ideology of the Revolution seriously, the counter-revolutionary discourse encompassed rejection of the text the revolutionaries were most proud of. In this manner it became a fundamental intellectual current, laying the groundwork for much of the modern conservative position.

The second reactionary wave was much less self-consciously counter-revolutionary or, at this juncture, counter-reformist than the first. Few writers specifically proclaimed the objective of rolling back the advances of popular participation in politics that were achieved through extensions of the franchise in the nineteenth century. One can nevertheless *construct* an ideological counter-movement out of several influential currents that arose at about the time when the major breakthroughs in the struggle for the extension of the franchise occurred. From the last third of the nineteenth century to the First World War and beyond, a vast and diffuse literature—embracing philosophy, psychology, politics, and *belles-lettres*—amassed every conceivable argument for disparaging the 'masses', the majority, parliamentary rule, and democratic government. Even though it made few proposals for alternative institutions, much of this literature implicitly or explicitly warned of the dire dangers threatening society as a result of the trend to democratization. With the benefit of hindsight, it is easy to argue that such writings shared in the responsibility for the destruction of democracy in Italy and Germany during the interwar period. To the extent the claim is justified, the second reaction must be given credit, if that is the correct term, for having produced history's most striking instance of the self-fulfilling prophecy. Curiously, the reaction that was least consciously intent on rolling back the ongoing trends or reforms became the one to have, or to be later accused of having had, the most destructive impact.

Now to the third reactionary wave: the contemporary critique of the welfare state and the attempts to roll back or 'reform' some of its provisions. These topics need not, perhaps, be gone over at this point. As direct, day-to-day observers of this movement we have a certain common-sense understanding of what is involved. At the same time, while a very large literature has by now criticized every aspect of the welfare state from the economic and political points of view, and in spite of determined assaults upon social welfare programmes and institutions by a variety of powerful political forces, it is too early to appraise the outcome of this new reactionary wave.

Three 'reactionary' theses

As will be apparent from this brief account, the size of my topic is enormous. In trying to get hold of it, I must be severely selective. It is therefore useful to point out immediately what I am *not* attempting. In the first place, I am not delving into the nature and deep roots of conservative thought. Rather, my aim is to delineate formal types of argument or rhetoric, and my emphasis will thus be on the major polemical postures and manœuvres likely to be engaged in by those who set out to debunk and roll back 'progressive' policies and movements of ideas. Second, I am not going to embark on a historical retelling of the successive reforms and counter-reforms since the French Revolution. Rather, I shall focus on common or typical arguments unfailingly made by each of the three reactive movements just noted.

Which are the arguments and how many are there? I must have an inbred urge toward symmetry. In canvassing for the principal ways of criticizing, assaulting, and ridiculing the three successive 'progressive' thrusts of Marshall's story I have come up with another triad: that is, with three principal reactive-reactionary theses which I call the perversity thesis, the futility thesis, and the jeopardy thesis. Let me explain briefly what I mean by each.

The perversity thesis, or thesis of the perverse effect, is closely connected with the semantic origin of the term 'reaction'. The coupling of 'action' and 'reaction' came into current usage as a result of Newton's third law of motion, which asserted that 'to every Action there is always opposed an equal Reaction'. Having thus been singled out for distinction in the then highly prestigious science of mechanics, the two concepts spilled over to other realms and were widely used in the analysis of society and history in the eighteenth century.[3]

No derogatory meaning whatsoever was attached at first to the term 'reaction'. The remarkably durable infusion of this meaning took place during the French Revolution and, specifically, after its great watershed, the events of Thermidor.[4] The fundamental reason is that the spirit of the Enlightenment, with its belief in the forward march of history, survived the Revolution, even among its critics, notwithstanding the Terror and other mishaps. One could deplore the excesses of the Revolution and yet continue to believe both in history's fundamentally progressive design and in the Revolution's being part of it. Such must have been the dominant contemporary attitude. Otherwise it would be hard to explain why those who 'reacted' to the Revolution in a predominantly negative manner came to be perceived and denounced as 'reactionaries'.

The semantic exploration of 'reaction' points straight to an important characteristic of 'reactionary' thinking. Because of the stubbornly progressive temper of the modern era, 'reactionaries' live in a hostile world. They are up against an intellectual climate in which a positive value attaches to whatever lofty objective is placed on the social agenda by self-proclaimed 'progressives'. Given this state of public opinion, reactionaries are not likely to launch an all-out attack on that objective. Rather, they will endorse it, sincerely or otherwise, but then attempt to demonstrate that the action proposed or undertaken is ill-conceived; indeed, they will often urge that this action will produce, via a series of unintended consequences, the exact opposite of the objective that is being pursued.[5]

This, then, is the perversity thesis. It argues that the attempt to push society in a particular direction will certainly result in its moving, but in the opposite direction. This thesis of the perverse effect of human action is remarkably simple, intriguing, and devastating if true. It is often referred to as the counter-intuitive or counter-productive effect of allegedly progressive public policies: attempts to reach for liberty will make society sink into slavery, the quest for democracy will produce oligarchy and tyranny, and social-welfare programmes will create more, rather than less, poverty. *Everything backfires.*

The second 'reactionary' argument, to which I shall devote the bulk of this essay, is what I call the futility thesis. While the thesis of the perverse effect proclaims that the alleged progress will in fact lead to regress, the futility thesis asserts, quite dissimilarly, that the attempt at change is abortive, that in one way or another any change is, was, or will be largely surface, façade, cosmetic, hence illusory, as the 'deep' structures of society remain wholly untouched.

It is significant that the French, rich in revolutionary experiences as they are, should have given this argument its classic epigrammatic expression, 'plus ça change plus c'est la même chose', in the aftermath of a revolution. The French journalist Alphonse Karr coined it in 1849, upon declaring that 'after so much upheaval and change it is about time to take note of this elementary truth'. Instead of a 'law of motion' we have here a law of no motion. Turning it into a strategy for avoiding change yields the well-known paradox of the Baron of Lampedusa in his novel *The Leopard*: 'If we want everything to stay as it is everything has to change.' Both conservatives and, even more, revolutionaries have eagerly adopted this aphorism from Sicilian society as the leitmotif or epigraph for studies that affirm the failure and futility of reform. But it is not only reform that stands accused of failing to bring real change: as was just noted, revolution, or any upheaval, can be similarly faulted, as is attested by one of the best-known (and best) jokes that came out of Eastern Europe after the installation of Communist regimes there in the wake of the Second World War: 'What is the difference between capitalism and socialism?' went the question. And the answer: 'In capitalism, man exploits man; in socialism it's the other way round.' Here was an effective way of asserting that nothing basic had changed in spite of the thorough transformation.

The perversity and futility arguments have something in common: both are remarkably bald. Therein lies, of course, much of their appeal. In both cases it is shown how actions undertaken to achieve a certain purpose miserably fail to do so: either no change occurs at all or the action yields an outcome that is the opposite of the one intended. Then there is a third, more moderate way of arguing against a change which, because of the prevailing state of public opinion, one does not care to attack head-on. This one asserts that to move in a certain direction, though perhaps desirable in itself, involves unacceptable costs or consequences of one sort or another. The trouble with this argument is that it normally involves a difficult and subjective comparison of highly heterogeneous benefits and costs; it will therefore carry less general conviction than a demonstration that an intended change is simply abortive or counter-productive.

The comparison of costs and benefits becomes rather more homogeneous and therefore more compelling when it takes a special, privileged form: that of focusing on a new reform in re-lation to one that has already been accomplished. If it can be argued that the two reforms are in some sense competitive or mutually exclusive so that the older reform will be endangered by the new one, then an element of comparability enters into the argument and the evaluation can proceed in vaguely common 'coins of progress': does it make sense to sacrifice the old progress for the new one? The older, hard-won conquests or accomplishments, so it is argued, are still fragile, still need to be consolidated, and will be placed in jeopardy by the new programme. I therefore call this argument the jeopardy thesis. It involves a more complex, historically grounded argument than the other two and is probably the most sophisticated of the three theses.

In line with the tripartite division of citizenship into the civil, political, and socio-economic dimensions, the jeopardy thesis should make its *first*, fully articulated appearance with the *second* reactionary wave, the one that criticizes the extension of the franchise and of democracy. It will be claimed that this extension imperils the earlier conquest of individual liberty, that undue in-sistence on participation or 'positive liberty' represents a danger for precious 'negative liberty'. Next, as the jeopardy thesis is used against the welfare state, it can deploy a double-barrelled argument. The welfare state, so it will be contended, is likely to endanger earlier advances with regard to individual rights (the first dimension of citizenship) and also with regard to democratic governance (the second, nineteenth-century dimension). All of these arguments have indeed surfaced in profusion.

So much by way of an overview of my project.*

The futility thesis

The difference between the perversity and the futility theses is clear-cut. The perverse effect asserts that, as a result of policies intending to push society in a certain direction, society moves, but in the *opposite* direction. According to the futility thesis, on the contrary, society does not move *at all* when an attempt is made to introduce change. In this manner the claims of the futility thesis seem more moderate than those of the perverse effect, but they are in reality more insulting to the 'change agents'. As long as the social world moves at all in response to human action for change, be it even in the wrong direction, hope remains that it can somehow be steered correctly. But the demonstration or discovery that such action is incapable of 'making a dent' at all leaves the promoters of change humiliated and demoralized.†

---

* I should add that the arguments, particularly the perversity and futility theses, are not the exclusive property of 'reactionaries'. Most generally these arguments will be made by groups who are out of power and oppose or criticize actions, any kind of actions, that are proposed or have already been taken. Whenever reactionaries find themselves in power and are able to carry out their own programmes and policies, they may in turn be attacked by 'liberals' or 'progressives' along the lines of the perversity or futility theses, whenever one or the other can be plausibly invoked. The conservative thesis can thus be made to generate certain stereotypical 'progressive' arguments.

† The perversity and futility arguments are compared at greater length later in this essay.

Questioning the extent of change wrought by the French Revolution:
Tocqueville

The perversity and futility theses are likely to appear with different
time-lags in relation to the social changes or movements which they
gloss. The perverse-effect argument can usually be made soon after
those changes have taken place. But the events have to be at some
distance before an interpretation can be brought forward implying
that the contemporaries of those events were far wrong when they
claimed them as fundamental change.

The French Revolution is a particularly striking illustration of
this point. Contemporaries, both in France and elsewhere, experienced it as an absolutely cataclysmic event—witness Burke's
phrase, early in the *Reflections*, 'All circumstances taken together,
the French Revolution is the most astonishing that has hitherto
happened in the world.' It is not surprising, therefore, that any
questioning of the Revolution's key role in shaping modern France
in all of its aspects had to wait for the passing of the revolutionary
generation. Such questioning came in 1856 when Tocqueville
presented the thesis, in his *L'Ancien Régime et la Révolution*, that the
Revolution represented much less of a break with the *ancien régime*
than had commonly been thought and that a number of highly
touted 'conquests' of the Revolution, from administrative centralization to widespread owner-operated small-scale farming, were in
fact already in place before its outbreak. Even the famous 'Rights of
Man and Citizen', so he tried to show, had, in part, already been
instituted by the *ancien régime*, long before they had been solemnly
'declared' in August 1789.

This debunking thesis of the book was widely taken as its
principal original contribution upon publication. One important
reviewer wrote:

> Astonishment grips us as we come to see through the book of M.
> de Tocqueville to what an extent almost all the things that we look
> upon as the results or, as the saying goes, the 'conquests' of the
> Revolution existed already in the *ancien régime*: administrative

centralization, administrative tutelage, administrative habits, guarantees of the civil servant ... extreme division of land, all of this is prior to 1789.... Reading those things one wonders what the Revolution has changed and why it has happened.[6]

In addition to his many other (and greater) glories, Tocqueville may thus be considered the originator of the futility thesis. Futility took a special 'progressive' shape here. Tocqueville did not deny that a number of basic social changes had been achieved in France by the end of the eighteenth century; but he argued that this had largely happened prior to the Revolution. Considering the huge travail of the Revolution, such a position was, to repeat, more stinging and insulting to pro-revolutionary opinion than the direct assaults of a Burke, a Maistre, or a Bonald. These authors at least gave credit to the Revolution for having brought forth large-scale changes and accomplishments, be they evil and disastrous. With Tocqueville's analysis, the titanic struggles and immense convulsions of the Revolution become strangely deflated, even puzzling and a bit ridiculous in retrospect as one is made to wonder what all the fuss was about.

Noting how the historiographical tradition has clung to the image of the Revolution as a total break (which was also the image the Revolution had of itself), François Furet puts the matter sharply: 'Into this mirror game where historian and Revolution take each other's word for it ... Tocqueville introduced doubt at the deepest level: what if, in this discourse about the break, there were nothing but the *illusion* of change?'[7]

These observations may help with another, smaller riddle: why Tocqueville's considerable contribution to the historiography of the French Revolution has been so largely neglected in France, in spite of the book's initial publishing success. It is only recently, in fact, that his work has been given extensive attention by a major French historian, Furet himself. The reason for the odd neglect cannot be just that, in France, Tocqueville was long perceived as a conservative or 'reactionary' by a milieu whose sympathies were predominantly with the Revolution and the left. The stance of

Hippolyte Taine was far more hostile to the Revolution than Tocqueville's, yet his *Origines de la France contemporaine* was taken most seriously by Aulard and other practitioners of the craft. Perhaps it was Tocqueville's espousal of the futility thesis that was responsible. Later historians never quite forgave him for having raised doubts about the *pivotal* character of the French Revolution: the phenomenon to whose study they were, after all, devoting their life.

Questioning the extent of change likely to follow from universal suffrage: Mosca and Pareto

Because the French Revolution was such a spectacular event, the dust had to settle before a deflating or debunking exercise such as Tocqueville's could be undertaken. The situation is quite different for the next appearance of the futility thesis, in reaction to the spread of the franchise and the consequent mass participation in politics during the second half of the nineteenth century. This spread occurred incrementally, unevenly, and rather unspectacularly among the various European countries and lasted for almost a century, if the count starts with the British Reform Act of 1832. There was no obvious stopping point on the march to universal suffrage which soon appeared to contemporary observers as the inevitable outcome of the process. Under the circumstances the trend was subjected to criticism long before it had run its course, and a whole band of detractors came forward. Some, such as the crowd analysts and Le Bon in particular, predicted outright disaster; others, again the 'cooler', more acerbic kind, opted for the futility thesis. They exposed and derided the illusions eternally naïve progressives were entertaining about the profound and beneficent changes that were supposed to flow from universal suffrage and maintained that, on the contrary, universal suffrage would change very little, if anything.

As with Tocqueville's thesis about the French Revolution, this seems a difficult position to argue. How could it be that the introduction of universal suffrage into still profoundly hierarchical societies would *not* have considerable consequences? The position could be maintained only by asserting that the reformers were ignoring some 'law' or 'scientific fact' that would make basic societal arrangements impervious to the proposed political change. This was the famous maxim, put forward in different forms by Gaetano Mosca (1858–1941) and Vilfredo Pareto (1848–1923), that any society, no matter what may be its 'surface' political organization, is always divided between the rulers and the ruled (Mosca) or between the élite and the non-élite (Pareto). The proposition was tailor-made to prove the futility of any move toward true 'political citizenship' via the franchise.

Starting from different premises, Mosca and Pareto had come, more or less independently, to the same conclusion towards the latter part of the nineteenth century. In the case of Mosca, the immediate 'sense data' by which he was surrounded as a young man in Sicily may have made it palpable to him that the mere extension of the right to vote would be rendered innocuous and meaningless by the island's powerfully entrenched landlords and other power holders. Perhaps it was the seeming absurdity of introducing what was an imported reform into a totally inhospitable milieu that led him to his basic point, first put forward at age 26 in *Teorica dei governi e governo parlamentare,* a book which he was then to rework, fatten up, and sometimes water down for the rest of his long life. This was the simple, almost obvious observation that all organized societies consist of a vast majority without any political power and a small minority of power holders: the 'political class', a term still used in Italy today. This insight—'a golden key to the arcana of human history' as Mosca's English editor put it in an introduction to his best-known work—was then put to a number of major doctrinal and polemical uses.[8]

First, Mosca claimed with great relish that the major political philosophers, from Aristotle to Machiavelli and Montesquieu, had only focused on the *superficial* characteristics of political regimes when they made those hoary distinctions between diverse forms of government, such as monarchies and republics, or aristocracies and democracies. All of these forms were shown to be subject to the far more fundamental rulers–ruled dichotomy. To build up at last a true science of politics, the essential task was to understand how the political class recruits itself, maintains itself in power, and legitimizes itself through ideologies which Mosca called 'political formulas', such as 'Divine Will', 'the People's Mandate', and similar transparent manœuvres.

Having debunked his illustrious predecessors, Mosca proceeded to take apart his contemporaries and their various proposals for the improvement of society. The power of his new conceptual tool is strikingly illustrated by his discussion of socialism. It starts with the seemingly unassuming sentence, 'Communist and collectivist societies would beyond any doubt be managed by officials.' As Mosca notes sarcastically, the socialists have conveniently forgotten this detail, which is decisive for a correct evaluation of the proposed social arrangements: in conjunction with the proscription of independent economic and professional activities, the rule of these powerful officials is bound to result in a state where a 'single, crushing, all-embracing, all-engrossing tyranny will weigh upon all'.[9]

Mosca's principal interest was in his own country and its political prospects. After the brief enthusiasm of the Risorgimento, the Italian intellectual and professional classes were greatly disappointed over the clientelistic politics that emerged in the newly united nation, particularly in the south. Armed with his new insight and given his special concern for that region, Mosca set out to prove once and for all that the (still quite imperfect) democratic institutions Italy had given itself were nothing but a sham. Here is his explanation:

> The legal assumption that the representative is chosen by the majority of voters forms the basis of our form of government. Many people blindly believe in its truth. Yet, the facts reveal something totally different. . . . Whoever has taken part in an election knows perfectly well that the *representative is not elected by the voters but, as a rule, has himself elected by them* . . . a candidacy is always the work of . . . an organized minority which inevitably forces its will upon the disorganized majority.[10]

The futility thesis could not be stated more clearly. The suffrage cannot change anything about the existing structure of power in society. 'He who has eyes to see'—one of Mosca's favourite expressions—must realize that 'the legal or rational basis of any political system that admits the masses of the people to representation is *a lie*.'[11]

Mosca's case against the emerging democratic institutions is remarkably different from that of his contemporary Gustave Le Bon. Mosca sees those institutions as impotent, as exercises in futility and hypocrisy; his attitude toward them and their advocates is one of ridicule and contempt. Le Bon, on the contrary, views the rise of the suffrage and of democratic institutions as ominous and dangerous because they will enhance the power of the crowd, with its unreason and its propensity to fall prey to demagogic *meneurs*.

Yet the two theses are not wholly separate. After arguing that the franchise would be unable to produce the positive changes its naïve advocates were counting on or hoping for, Mosca managed to adduce several reasons why it might actually make things worse. In other words, he slipped from the futility to the perversity thesis. He thought, for example, that the malpractices that come with the manipulation of elections on the part of the political class would make the quality of candidates for public office deteriorate and would thereby discourage higher-minded citizens from taking an interest in public affairs.[12]

Pareto's theory of élite domination as a constant of history is close to that of Mosca, both in its analysis and in the polemical uses to which it is put. In the *Cours d'économie politique* (1896–97) Pareto's language sounds at first curiously, perhaps consciously, like the *Communist Manifesto*: 'The struggle undertaken by certain individuals to appropriate for themselves the wealth produced by others is the great fact that dominates the whole history of humanity.'[13] But in the same paragraph Pareto distances himself from Marxism by using the term 'spoliation' rather than 'exploitation' or 'surplus' and by making it clear that spoliation is due to the dominant class obtaining control of the state, which is called a 'machine for spoliation'. The crucial, Mosca-like result follows immediately: 'it matters but little whether the ruling class is an oligarchy, a plutocracy, or a democracy'.[14]

The point Pareto is really after here is that a democracy can be just as 'spoliative' of the mass of people as any other regime. He notes that the method by which the ruling or spoliating class is recruited has nothing to do with the fact or degree of spoliation itself; he intimates in fact that when élite recruitment proceeds by means of democratic elections rather than by heredity or by co-option, the chances for spoliation of the mass may well be larger.[15]

According to Pareto, the advent of universal suffrage and of democratic elections could not, therefore, bring any real social or political change. This position dovetails remarkably with his work on the distribution of income which made him instantly famous among economists when he first published it in 1896. Soon after assuming his Lausanne chair in 1893, Pareto assembled data on the frequency distributions of individual incomes in various countries at different epochs and went on to demonstrate that all of these distributions followed rather closely a simple mathematical expression relating the number of income receivers above a given income to that income. Moreover, the principal parameter in that expression turned out to have very similar numerical values for all the distributions that had been collected. These results suggested to both Pareto and his contemporaries that he had discovered a natural law. Pareto actually wrote, 'we are here in the presence of a natural law'[16]—and his findings became widely known as 'Pareto's Law'. The authoritative, contemporary encyclopedia of economics, *Palgrave's Dictionary of Political Economy* (London: Macmillan, 1926), carried an entry under this heading, written by the renowned economist F. Y. Edgeworth.

Pareto's success was soon emulated. In 1911, the sociologist Robert Michels, who had been considerably influenced by both Mosca and Pareto, proclaimed an 'Iron Law of Oligarchy' in his book *Political Parties*. According to Michels, political parties, trade unions and other mass organizations are invariably ruled by largely self-serving and self-perpetuating oligarchies, defying attempts at democratic control or participation.

Once Pareto had elevated his statistical findings about income distribution to the status of a natural law, considerable policy implications followed. It could now be claimed that, just as in the case of interference with the law of supply and demand, it was futile (at best) to attempt to change so basic and invariant an aspect of the economy as the distribution of income, whether through expropriation, taxation, or social-welfare legislation.

The new law's principal polemical use was probably in controverting the socialists whose electoral fortunes were then on the rise in many countries. As the editor of Pareto's collected works comments:

> how fine a challenge to demonstrate, documents in hand, that the distribution of incomes is determined by fundamental forces...! If the enterprise were crowned with success the solutions advocated by socialism would definitely be classed as utopias.[17]

The polemical emphasis is on the naïveté of those who wish to change what is given as invariant by nature. But again, as in Mosca's analysis, the argument is enriched by a dash of the perverse effect. To go against the natural order of things is not just unavailing; for, as Pareto writes in an article of vulgarization:

> The efforts made by state socialism to change artificially this [income] distribution have as first effect a destruction of wealth. They result therefore in exactly the opposite of what one was after: they worsen the condition of the poor instead of improving it.[18]

Apparently the authors of the futility thesis are not quite comfortable with their own argument: whenever possible, they look to the perverse effect for reinforcement, adornment, and closure. Even Lampedusa, master-strategist of social immobility, predicts toward the end of his novel that immobility will, in due course, be followed by deterioration: 'Later it will be different, but worse. We were the Leopards, the Lions: we will be replaced by the little chacals, the hyenas...'.

Questioning the extent to which the welfare state actually 'delivers the goods' to the poor

The conservative critique of the welfare state is principally grounded in traditional economic reasoning about markets, the equilibrium properties of market outcomes, and the harmful consequences of interfering with these outcomes. The critique has pointed to the various unfortunate and counter-productive effects likely to follow from transfer payments to the unemployed, the disadvantaged and, in general, the poor. However well-intentioned, such payments are alleged to encourage 'sloth and depravity', to foster dependency, to destroy other more constructive support systems, and to 'mire' the poor in their poverty. This is the perverse effect of interferences with the market.

Yet, for this effect to come into operation, the welfare state must have at least one prior accomplishment to its credit: to generate the transfer payments and to have them actually *reach* the poor. Only upon this coming to pass can the unhappy consequences (of sloth, dependency, and so on) actually unfold.

At this point the outline of another possible critique emerges: what if the transfer payments never reach the intended beneficiaries and are diverted instead, not perhaps wholly but in large part, to other social groups with more clout?

The argument has much in common with the Mosca–Pareto denunciation of democratic elections as a meaningless sham. It has the insulting quality which was noted earlier as a characteristic feature of the futility thesis. When a welfare scheme can be shown to benefit the middle class instead of reaching the poor, its promoters are exposed not just as naïvely unaware of conceivable perverse side-effects; rather, they will come under the suspicion of being self-serving either by promoting the scheme from the start with the intent of feathering their own nest or, somewhat more charitably, by *learning* to divert a good part of the funds, once available, to their own pockets.

Clearly, to the extent that this sort of argument could be marshalled with some degree of plausibility, it would make a devastating case. The claims on behalf of the welfare state would be shown up as fraudulent and it would be its critics who, rather than appearing to lack in compassion, would be able to pose as the real defenders of the poor against grasping, parasitic special interests.

However attractive it may be for the opponents of welfare-state legislation to invoke this argument, the extent to which it has actually been used in recent years has been limited. There are two principal reasons. First, this time the futility thesis is too obviously inconsistent with the perverse-effect argument. It requires special gifts of sophistry to argue at one and the same time that welfare payments have those highly advertised perverse effects on the behaviour pattern of the poor *and* that they do not reach these same poor. The second reason is specific to the debate in the United States. The principal debate on welfare reform has here been concerned with those programmes—primarily Aid to Families with Dependent Children (AFDC)—whose beneficiaries have to pass through a means test; in the absence of vast mismanagement or corruption, the likelihood of such programmes being diverted to the non-poor is rather small. Consequently the main burden of the economic and political case against the welfare state has to be carried by other arguments.

The futility or 'diversion' argument has nevertheless played an important subsidiary role in the debate. This was particularly evident during the days of Lyndon Johnson's 'Great Society', when the charge was often heard that many of the newer social-welfare programmes served primarily to provide jobs to a large group of administrators, social workers, and sundry professionals who were pictured as power-hungry bureaucrats forever straining to expand their bureaux and perquisites. The means-tested welfare programmes, whose disbursements to the poor normally escape, as just noted, the strictures of the diversion argument, are actually quite vulnerable to it inasmuch as their administration is more labour-intensive than is the case for the categorical, insurance-type programmes where eligibility is triggered by fairly clear-cut events or criteria, such as age, loss of job, accident, or sickness.

The futility thesis, in the shape of the just-noted diversion argument, has, on occasion, been put forward as a general critique of the welfare state. An early example is a brief but influential article by George Stigler, Nobel-Prize-winning economist from Chicago, in 1970. It was entitled, a bit mysteriously, 'Director's Law of Public Income Redistribution'.[19] Director, it turns out, is the name of a fellow Chicago economist (Aaron Director, Milton Friedman's brother-in-law), whom Stigler credits with having enunciated a 'law'—probably in conversation, as no reference is given or can be found in Director's published writings. According to Stigler, Director held that 'public expenditures are made for the primary benefit of the middle classes, and financed with taxes which are borne in considerable part by the poor and rich'. Early in his article, Stigler forgets about the rich and bends the 'Law' to mean that public expenditures for such purposes as education, housing, social security, and so on, largely represent, if considered in conjunction with the taxes that finance them, state-mandated income transfers from the poor to the middle class. How can such a state of affairs come about in a democracy? Simple, says Stigler. The middle class first manœuvres the voting system so as to reduce turnout of the poor by means of literacy and registration requirements and the like; once in control of political power, it moulds the fiscal system so as to suit its corporate interests. Stigler also cites some empirical evidence: higher education, in California and elsewhere, is subsidized by the state out of general revenue, but the benefits of the university system accrue mostly to the children of the middle and upper classes; similarly, police protection serves primarily the propertied classes; and so on.

This sort of argument is of course familiar from the Marxist tradition which, at least in its more primitive or 'vulgar' version, views the state as the 'Executive Committee of the bourgeoisie' and denounces any claim that it may conceivably serve the general or public interest as so much hypocrisy. It comes as something of a surprise to encounter so 'subversive' a reasoning among certain pillars of the 'free enterprise' system. But this is not the first time that shared hatreds have made for strange bedfellowship. The hatred that is being shared in this case is directed against the attempt at reforming some unfortunate or unjust features of the capitalist system through public intervention and programmes. On the left, such programmes are criticized because it is feared that any success they might have would reduce revolutionary zeal. On the right, or among the more orthodox economists, they are subject to criticism and mockery because any intervention by the state, and particularly any increase in public expenditure for purposes other than law, order, and defence, is considered as noxious or futile interference with a system that is supposed to be self-equilibrating.

Stigler's 'Director's Law' was to be frequently invoked, with or without acknowledgement, in the subsequent years of stepped-up assault on the welfare state.

There are of course a number of instances that exhibit consider-able 'beneficial involvement of the non-poor in the operation of the welfare state', to use the apt expression of a British publication that analyses and criticizes the phenomenon from the left.[20] But the way the story unfolds often departs significantly from the Director–Stigler script. A good example is a welfare programme that has been prominent in Latin America.

In view of the massive influx of the rural population into Latin American cities, low-cost public or subsidized housing programmes were undertaken in many countries, starting in the 1950s. Initially the housing units built by these programmes were, almost every-where, far too expensive for the poorer families whose housing needs they were supposed to address. In consequence, this housing became available primarily to the middle or lower-middle class. A number of factors contributed to this outcome: desire, on the part of politicians, to be seen 'entregando una casa bonita' (handing over a nice-looking house); ignorance among the planners and archi-tects of the projects about the kind of housing poor people could afford; unavailability of low-cost materials and building methods; and, particularly in the tropical zone, the alternative, open to the poor, to build their own homes, with their own labour, from a variety of very cheap, discarded, or 'found' materials, on 'free' land (obtained through squatting). Subsequent programmes to help the poor with their housing needs learned from this experience and were more successful in reaching the truly poor. For example, municipal authorities or housing agencies sponsored so-called 'sites-and-services' programmes: public provision and financing were limited to making available basic utilities on properly sub-divided lots on which the occupants were left to build their homes by means of their own effort. Finally, public assistance to housing came to be seen as most useful if it concentrated on providing public transportation and basic utilities for already built-up neigh-bourhoods, however 'substandard' and ripe for the bulldozer they seemed to the eyes of middle-class observers.

A number of observations are in order. First of all, even the housing that was unsuitable for the poor accomplished a genuine social purpose as it extended relief to the hard-pressed lower-middle class in Latin American cities. Secondly, building low-cost housing and being criticized for its shortcomings became a valuable learning experience for public officials and housing agencies. It helped them to visualize the real dimensions of urban poverty. Eventually, traditional images about 'solutions' to the 'housing problem'—largely imported from the more advanced countries—were reshaped and methods of public intervention were devised that had more of a chance of reaching the elusive 'poorest of the poor'.

It appears, then, that the story of the beneficial involvement of the not-so-poor in programmes meant for the poor is both more complex *and* less cynical than is implied in the version which attri-butes the diversion of funds wholly to the greater clout or elbow power of the better-off. In particular, critical analysis of results achieved and 'anomalies' encountered by officials, social scientists, and other observers can play an important corrective role in a continuing process of policy-making.

Further reflections on the futility thesis

Futility compared with perversity   During each of our three epi-sodes the futility argument amounted to a *denial or downplaying of change* in the face of such seemingly enormous, epochal movements as the French Revolution, the trend towards universal suffrage and democratic institutions during the latter part of the nineteenth century, and the emergence and expansion of the welfare state subsequently. The appeal of the arguments largely rests on the remarkable feat of contradicting, often with obvious relish, the common-sense understanding of these events as replete with upheaval, change or real reform.

A considerable similarity in reasoning appears particularly between two of our episodes, that is, the critique of democracy, at the hands of Mosca and Pareto, and the critique of the welfare-state policies, on the part of Stigler and his followers. In both cases, attempts at political or economic change or reform are shown to come to naught because they disregard some 'law' whose existence has allegedly been ascertained by social science. The ambition to democratize power in society through the establishment of universal suffrage is laughable in the eyes of Pareto, who had investigated the distribution of income and wealth and had found that it follows everywhere an invariant, highly unequal pattern that came to be known as Pareto's Law. With income being distributed in this law-given manner, and with ancient hierarchies having been dismantled by the bourgeois age, it was obvious to Pareto that modern society was in reality a plutocracy: a favourite term of his, jointly with 'spoliation'. Vaunted democracy was nothing but a mask hiding the reality of plutocracy. In turn, Robert Michels's 'Iron Law of Oligarchy' was closely modelled on the ideas of Mosca and Pareto, and Director's Law, as enunciated by Stigler, can similarly be viewed as descending directly from the constructions of Pareto and Michels.

At this point a substantial difference between the perversity and the futility theses must be noted. At first sight it might seem that the futility thesis, as well as the perverse effect, is based on the notion of unanticipated consequences of human action. Only, when futility rather than perversity is invoked, the unintended side-effects simply cancel out the original action instead of going so far as to produce a result that is the opposite of the one that was intended. But the futility thesis is not constructed in this way, as though it were simply a milder version of the perversity thesis. In its case, human actions or intentions are frustrated, not because they unleash a series of side-effects, but because they pretend to change the unchangeable, because they ignore the basic structures of society. The two theses are therefore based on almost opposite views of the social universe and of purposive human and social action. The perverse effect sees the social world as remarkably volatile, with every move leading immediately to a variety of unsuspected countermoves; the futility advocates, on the contrary, view the world as highly structured and as evolving according to immanent laws, which human actions are laughably incapable of modifying.

It is not surprising, then, that the two theses have very different ideological affinities. In Maistre's classic formulation of the perverse effect, it is Divine Providence that foils the human actors. By bringing about an outcome that is the exact opposite of human intentions, it almost seems to take a *personal* interest and delight in 'sweet revenge' and in demonstrating human impotence. When it comes to the futility thesis, human actions are mocked and frustrated without this sort of personal pique: they are shown to be irrelevant as they run foul of some majestic law that rules impersonally. In this manner the perverse effect has an affinity to myth and religion and to the belief in direct supernatural intervention into human affairs whereas the futility argument is more tied to the subsequent belief in the authority of science and particularly to the nineteenth-century aspiration to construct a social science with laws as solid as those that were then believed to rule the physical universe.

The trouble with futility The futility thesis thrives on 'unmasking' or 'exposing', on demonstrating the inconsistency between proclaimed purposes (establishment of democratic institutions or of redistributive welfare programmes) and actual practice (continued oligarchic rule or mass poverty). The trouble with the argument is that futility is proclaimed too soon. The first evidence that a programme is being stymied or deflected by existing structures and interests is seized upon. There is a rush to judgement and no allowance is made for social learning or for incremental, corrective policy-making. Quite unlike the admirably reflective social scientist, societies and their policy-makers are taken to lack wholly the ability to engage in self-evaluation; they are also assumed to have an infinite capacity for tolerating what is usually known as hypocrisy, that is, inconsistency between proclaimed values and actual practice.

The main charge against the futility thesis must therefore be that it does not take itself and its own effects on events seriously enough. The story it tells about a wide and ever-widening gulf between proclaimed goals and actual social outcomes cannot possibly end there. As the story is absorbed by the listeners, it sets up a tension and thus activates a dynamic that is either self-fulfilling or self-refuting. The dynamic is self-fulfilling when the assertions about the meaninglessness of intended changes and reforms weaken resistance and lead to their further emasculation and outright abandonment. In this sense Mosca and Pareto can be said to have contributed to the rise of Fascism in Italy by pouring ridicule and discredit on the country's fledgling democratic institutions. Alternatively, the dynamic will be self-refuting as the very tension set up by the futility claims makes for new, more determined, and better informed efforts at achieving real change. In this manner the futility thesis undergoes a notable transformation: it becomes, in effect, remarkably activist when its initial stance is that of a cool and mocking observer of human folly and self-deception; and whatever truth the thesis uncovers turns out to be ephemeral when it was so sure that its pronouncements were based on some unchangeable 'laws' of the social world.

Because of its contemptuous and debunking attitude towards 'purported' change and progress, the futility thesis belongs squarely in the conservative camp. It is indeed one of the principal weapons in the reactionary arsenal. As may already have been noticed, however, it has a close affinity to arguments coming from the other end of the political spectrum. The conjunction of radical and reactionary arguments is a special characteristic of the futility thesis.

Whereas the perverse-effect argument takes an extremely serious view of the political, social, or economic policies which it holds to be counter-productive, the futility thesis rather derides those attempts at change as inept. The existing social order is shown to be expert at reproducing itself; in the process, it defeats or co-opts many attempts at introducing change or progress. This is the point where the argument shows a striking family resemblance to radical reasoning. This has often taken progressives or reformers to task for ignoring basic 'structures' of the social system and for nourishing and propagating illusions about the possibility of introducing, without prior 'fundamental' changes in those structures, this or that 'partial' improvement, such as more democratic governance, universal primary education, or certain social-welfare programmes. If some such features are in fact legislated on, the next step is to argue that the pre-existing pattern of domination has not really changed: it has just become more intricate to figure out how it functions in spite of or perhaps because of the changes. At this point, heavy use is made of such metaphors as 'mask', 'veil' and 'disguise', and the radical social analysts, like their conservative counterparts, obligingly provide the service of lifting the veil, tearing off the mask, and making us see through the disguise.

It never seems to occur to these critics that the tension between the announced aims of a social programme and its actual effectiveness makes for a far more complex story than is conveyed by the contrast between mask and reality. The relationship that is implicit in this tired metaphor can, on occasion, change drastically, in line with the dialectic that some of the critics profess to admire: the so-called mask can manage to subvert the reality instead of hiding and preserving it. As was suggested by Kolakowski, the more appropriate metaphor is, in that case, the Nessus tunic of antiquity which burns him who puts it on.[21] In fact, through their denunciations of the gulf between announced policy objectives and reality, our conservative or radical critics are themselves busily weaving just such a garment. But perhaps it is better on the whole that they not be aware of this role, otherwise their fault-finding might lose in action-arousing effectiveness.

Just once in a while one would want to see them a little less bitter and mean-spirited.

Are All Tongues Equal? Language, Culture and National Identity

E. J. HOBSBAWM

Language, culture and national identity is the title of my essay but its central subject is the situation of languages in cultures, written or spoken languages still being the main medium of these. More specifically, my subject is 'multiculturalism' in so far as this depends on language. 'Nations' come into it since, in the states in which we all live, political decisions about how and where languages are used for public purposes (for example, in schools) are crucial. And these states are today commonly identified with 'nations' as in the term 'United Nations'. This is a dangerous confusion. So let me begin with a few words about it.

Since there are hardly any colonies left, practically all of us today live in independent and sovereign states. With rare exceptions, such as the 400 expelled Palestinians who camped in the no man's land between Israel and Lebanon, even exiles and refugees live in states, though not their own. It is fairly easy to get agreement about what constitutes such a state, at any rate the modern model of it which has become the template for all new independent political entities since the late eighteenth century. It is a territory, preferably co-herent and demarcated by frontier lines from its neighbours, within which *all* citizens, without exception, come under the exclusive rule of the territorial government and the rules under which it operates. Against this there is no appeal, except by authorization of that government; for even the superiority of European Union law over national law was established only by the decision of the constituent governments of the Union. Within the state's territory all who are born and live there are citizens except those specifically excluded as 'foreigners' by the state, which also has the power to admit people to citizenship; but not, in democratic states, to deprive them of it. Foreigners are taken to belong to some other territorial state, though the growth of inhumanity since the First World War has produced a growing, and now very large body of officially invisible denizens for whom special terms have had to be devised in our tragic century: 'stateless', '*apatride*', 'illegal immigrant', or whatever.

At some time, mainly since the end of the nineteenth century, the inhabitants of this state have been identified with an 'imagined community', bonded together, as it were, laterally by such things as language, culture, ethnicity and the like. The ideal of such a state is represented by an ethnically, culturally and linguistically homogeneous population. We now know that this standing invitation to 'ethnic cleansing' is dangerous, and completely unrealistic, for out of the almost 200 states today only about a dozen correspond to this programme. Moreover, it would have surprised the founders of the original nation-states. For them the unity of the nation was political and not socio-anthropological. It consisted in the decision of a sovereign people to live under common laws and a common constitution, irrespective of culture, language and ethnic composition. 'A nation', said the Abbé Sieyes, with habitual French lucidity, 'is the totality of individuals united by living under a common law and represented by the same legislative assembly.'[1] The assumption that communities of common ethnic descent, language, culture, religion and so on ought to find expression in territorial states, let alone in a single territorial state, was, of course, equally new. It could actually be a reversal of historic values, as in Zionism. In 1900 an orthodox rabbi wrote:

> Strangers have arisen who say that the people of Israel should be clothed in secular nationalism, a nation like all other nations, that Judaism rests on three things, national feeling, the land and the language, and that national feeling is the most praiseworthy element in the brew and the most effective in preserving Judaism, while the observance of the Torah and the commandments is a

private matter depending on the inclination of each individual. May the Lord rebuke these evil men and may He who chooseth Jerusalem seal their mouths.[2]

The Dzikover Rebbe, whom I have here quoted, undoubtedly represented the tradition of Judaism.

A third observation brings me closer to the main theme of this essay. The concept of a *single*, exclusive and unchanging ethnic, cultural or other identity is a dangerous piece of brainwashing. Human mental identities are not like shoes, of which we can only wear one pair at a time. We are all multi-dimensional beings. Whether a Mr Patel in London will think of himself primarily as an Indian, a British citizen, a Hindu, a Gujarati-speaker, an ex-colonist from Kenya, a member of a specific caste or kin-group, or in some other capacity, depends on whether he faces an immigration officer, a Pakistani, a Sikh or Moslem, a Bengali-speaker and so on. There is no single platonic essence of Patel. He is all these and more at the same time.

Historically, multiple identity lies behind even national homogeneity. Every German in the past, and vestigially even today, had simultaneously two or three identities: as a member of a tribe—the Saxons, the Swabians, the Franks—of a German principality or state, and of a linguistic culture combining a single, standard written language for all Germans, with a variety of spoken dialects, some of which also had begun to develop a written literature. (The Reformation brought not one but several Bible translations into German languages.) Indeed, until Hitler, people were regarded as Germans *by virtue of being* Bavarians, Saxons or Swabians, who could often understand one another only when they spoke the written, standard culture-language.

This brings me naturally to my central theme of multilingualism and multiculturalism. Both are historically novel as concepts. They could not arise until three circumstances had combined: the aspiration to universal literacy, the political mobilization of the common people, and a particular form of linguistic nationalism.

Historically the coexistence of peoples of different languages and cultures is normal; or rather, nothing is less common than countries inhabited exclusively by people of a single uniform language and culture. Even in Iceland, with its 300,000 inhabitants, such uniformity is only maintained by a ruthless policy of Iceland-ization, including forcing every immigrant to take an ancient Icelandic name.[3] At the time of the French Revolution only half the inhabitants of France could speak French and only 12–13 per cent spoke it 'correctly'. The extreme case is Italy, where, at the moment when it became a state, only two or three Italians out of a hundred actually used the Italian language at home. So long as most people lived in an oral universe, there was no necessary link between the spoken language and the written language of the literate minority. So long as reading and writing were strictly the affair of specialized minorities, it did not even have to be a living language. The admin-istration of India in the 1830s switched from written classical Persian, which nobody in India spoke, to written English, which was equally incomprehensible. If illiterates needed to communicate with those who spoke other languages, they relied on intermedi-aries who could speak the language, learned enough of the other language to get by, or developed pidgins or creoles which became unwritten but effective means of communication and have become a fashionable topic for study among linguists.

A single national language only became important when ordi-nary citizens became an important component of the state; and the written language had to have a relation to the spoken language only when these citizens were supposed to read and write it. But remem-ber that universal primary education, outside a few exceptional countries, is not much more than a century old.

The original case for a standard language was entirely democratic, not cultural. How could citizens understand, let alone take part in, the government of their country, if it was conducted in an incom-prehensible language—for example, in Latin, as in the Hungarian parliament before 1840? Would this not guarantee government by an élite minority? This was the argument of the Abbé Gregoire in 1794.[4] Education in French was, therefore, essential for French citizens, whatever the language they spoke at home. This remained essentially the position in the United States, another product of the same age of democratic revolution. To be a citizen, an immigrant had to pass a test in English, and readers of Leo Rosten's *The Education of Hyman Kaplan* will be familiar with this process of linguistic homogenization. I need not add that Mr Kaplan's struggles with the English language were not intended to stop him talking Yiddish with his wife at home, which he certainly did; nor did they affect his children, who obviously went to English-speaking local schools. What people spoke or wrote among themselves was nobody's business but their own, like their religion. It is notable that even in 1970—that is to say before the onset of the present wave of mass immigration—33 million Americans, plus an unknown percentage of another 9 million who didn't answer the relevant question, said that English was not their mother tongue. Over three quarters of them were second-generation or older, American-born.[5]

In practice, education in languages other than the standard national language was traditionally left to private effort, or to special voluntary provision by minority communities or by local option, as often happened in America. Thus bilingual education in English and German was introduced in Cincinnati in 1840. Most such arrangements—and there were several in the second half of the nineteenth century—had quietly faded away by the time the demand for official, federal, bilingual education surfaced in the 1960s and 1970s. Let me say that this was a *political* rather than an educational demand. It was part of the rise of a new kind of ethnic and identity politics during this period.

The situation was different, of course, where there was no single, predominant, national language, spoken or even written, or where a linguistic community resented the superior status of another language. In the multinational Habsburg empire 'the language of (public) office and school' became a political issue from 1848, as it did, somewhat later, in Belgium and Finland. The usual formula here was—and I quote the Hungarian Nationality Law of 1868— that people should be educated in their own language at primary school level, and, under certain circumstances, at secondary school level, and that they should be allowed to use it, directly or through interpreters, in dealings with public authorities. (But note that what was a language was *politically* defined. It did not include Yiddish, nor the creole spoken in Istria, where experts in the 1850s counted thirteen different national varieties.)

To have a language, as distinct from a dialect or 'jargon', you needed to be classified as a nation or nationality. The formula could work in areas of solid settlement by one language group, and local or even regional government could be substantially conducted in what was called the 'language of common use' (*Umgangsprache*), but it raised big problems in areas of mixed settlement and in most cities. The real educational issue, of course, was not primary but secondary and tertiary education. This is where the major battles were fought. Here the issue was not mass literacy but the linguistic status of unofficial élites. For we must remember that, until the Second World War, not more than 2 per cent of the age group 15–19 went on to higher education even in countries with a reputation for democracy like Denmark and the Netherlands. Under the circumstances, any Fleming or Finn who had got to university level was certainly capable of pursuing studies in French or Swedish. In short, once again the issue was not educational but political.

Basically this system of one official language per country became part of everyone's aspiration to become a nation-state, though special arrangements had to be made for minorities which insisted on them. Multilingual nations like Switzerland were regarded as freaks; but, given the great cantonal autonomy in that country, even Switzerland is hardly multilingual, because almost every canton is, in fact, monoglot. Colonies winning their independence after the Second World War automatically thought in terms of some home-grown national language as the basis of national education and culture: Urdu in Pakistan, Hindi in India, Sinhala in Sri Lanka, Arabic in Algeria. As I shall show in a moment, this was a dangerous delusion. Small peoples which define themselves ethnic-linguistically still hanker after this ideal of homogeneity: Latvia only for Lettish-speakers, Moldavia only for Romanians. As it so happens, in 1940, when this area once again passed to Russia, almost half its population consisted not of Romanians, but of Ukrainians, Russians, Bulgarians, Turks, Jews and a number of other groups.[6] Let us be clear: in the absence of a willingness to change languages, national linguistic homogeneity in multi-ethnic and multilingual areas can be achieved only by mass compulsion, expulsion or genocide. Poland, which had a third non-Polish population in 1939, is today overwhelmingly Polish, but only because its Germans were expelled to the west, its Lithuanians, Belorussians and Ukrainians were detached to form part of the USSR in the east, and its Jews were murdered. Let me add that neither Poland nor any other homogeneous country can stay homogeneous in the present world of mass labour migration, mass flight, mass travel and mass urbanization, except, once again, by ruthless exclusion or the creation *de jure* or *de facto* of apartheid societies.

The case for the privileged use of any language as the only language of education and culture in a country is thus political and ideological or, at best, pragmatic. Except in one respect, it is not educational. Universal literacy is extremely difficult to achieve in a written language that has no relation to the spoken vernacular; and it may be impossible, unless the parents and the community are particularly anxious for their children to become literate in that language, as is the case with most immigrants into anglophone countries today. Whether this requires formal bilingual education is another matter. Basically, the demand for official education in a language other than the already established one, when this does not bring obvious advantages to the learners, is a demand for recognition, for power or for status, not for easier learning. However, it may also be a demand for ensuring the survival and development of a non-competitive language otherwise likely to fade away. Whether official institutionalization is necessary to achieve this today is an interesting question, but, according to the best expert in the field, bilingual education alone won't do the trick.[7]

Let me just add one important point. Any language that moves from the purely oral to the realm of reading and writing—*a fortiori* any language that becomes a medium for schoolteaching or official use—changes its character. It has to be standardized in grammar, spelling, vocabulary and perhaps pronunciation, and its lexical range has to be extended to cover new needs. At least a third of the vocabulary of modern Hebrew has been formed in the twentieth century, since biblical Hebrew, rather like the Welsh of the *Mabinogion*, belonged to an ancient people of herdsmen and peasants. The established culture-languages of modern states— Italian, Spanish, French, English, German, Russian and one or two others—went through this phase of social engineering before the nineteenth century. Most of the world's written languages did so in the past hundred years, in so far as they were 'modernized', and some, like Basque, are still in the process of doing so. The very process of turning language into a medium for writing, destroys it as a vernacular. Suppose we say, as champions of African-Americans sometimes say: our kids should not be taught in standard English, which is a language they don't speak, but in their own black English, which is not a 'wrong' version of standard English, but an independent idiom of its own. So it may be; but if you turned it into a school language it would cease to be the language that the kids speak. A distinguished French historian, whose native language was Flemish, once said: 'the Flemish they now learn in school in Flanders is not the language the mothers and grandmothers of Flanders taught their children.' It was no longer a 'mother tongue' in the literal sense. A lady who looked after my apartment in New York, bilingual in Spanish and Galician, like all from her region in Spain, has difficulty in understanding the purified and standardized Gallego which is now an official language in Galicia. It is not the language of common use in the region, but a new social construct.

*   *   *

What I have said so far may be true or not, but it is now largely out-of-date. For three things have happened which were not thought of in the heyday of nationalism, and are still not thought of by the dangerous late-comers to nationalism. First, we no longer live entirely in a culture based on reading and writing. Second, we no longer live in a world where the idea of a single all-purpose national language is generally feasible; in other words, we live in a *necessarily* plurilingual world. And third, we live in an era when, at least for the time being, there is a single language for universal global communication, namely a version of English.

The first development is basically the effect of film, television but, above all, of the small portable radio. It means that spoken vernacular languages are no longer only face to face, domestic or restricted idioms. Illiterates are, therefore, directly within reach of the wider world and wider culture. This may also mean that small languages and dialects can survive more easily, in so far as even a modest population is enough to justify a local radio programme. Minority languages can thus be cheaply provided for. On the other hand exposure to some bigger language through the media may speed up linguistic assimilation. On balance, radio favours small languages, while TV has been hostile to them, but this may no longer be true when cable and satellite television are as accessible as FM radio.* In short, it is no longer necessary to make a language *official* for it to be moved out of the home and off the street into the wider world. Of course, none of this means that illiterates are not at a severe and growing disadvantage compared to literates, whether in written languages or in computer languages.

In Europe, national standard languages were usually based on a combination of dialects spoken by the main-state people, which was transformed into a literary idiom. In the post-colonial states this is rarely possible, and when it is, as in Sri Lanka, the results of giving Sinhalese exclusive official status have been disastrous. In fact, the most convenient 'national languages' are either a lingua franca or a pidgin developed purely for intercommunication between peoples who don't talk each other's languages, like Swahili, Filipino or Bahasa Indonesia, or former imperial languages like English in India and Pakistan. Their advantage is that they are neutral between the languages actually spoken, and hence put no one group at a

---

* In New York, in 1994, television programmes were available in Italian, French, Chinese, Japanese, Spanish, Polish, Greek and even occasionally in Albanian—though only at certain times of day, except for Spanish.

particular advantage or disadvantage: except, of course, the élite. The price India pays for conducting its affairs in English as an insurance against language-based civil wars such as that in Sri Lanka, is that people who have not had the several years full-time education which make a person fluent in a foreign written language will never make it above a relatively modest level in public affairs or—today—in business. That price is worth paying, I think. Nevertheless, imagine the effect on Europe if Hindi were the only language allowed in the European parliament, and both *The Times*, *Le Monde* and the *Frankfurter Allgemeine Zeitung* could be read only by those literate in Hindi.

All this is changing, or will profoundly change, the relation of languages to each other in multinational societies. The ambition of all languages in the past which aspired to the status of national languages and to be the basis of national education and culture was to be all-purpose languages at all levels (that is, interchangeable with the major culture-languages), especially, of course, with the dominant language against which they tried to establish themselves. Thus in Finland, Finnish was to be capable of replacing Swedish for all purposes, in Belgium Flemish of replacing French. Hence the real triumph of linguistic emancipation was to set up a vernacular university: in the history of Finland, Wales and the Flemish movement the date when such a university was established is a major date in nationalist history. A lot of smaller languages have tried to do this over the past centuries, starting, I suppose, with Dutch in the seventeenth century, and ending, so far, with Catalan. Some, like Basque, are still trying to do it.

In practice, this is now ceasing to be the case operationally, although small-nation nationalism does what it can to resist the trend. Languages once again have niches, and are used in different situations and for different purposes. Therefore they don't need to cover the same ground. This is partly because, for international purposes, only a few languages are actually used. Though the administration of the European Union spends one third of its income on translation from and into all the eleven languages which have official status, it is a safe bet that the overwhelming bulk of its actual work is conducted in not more than three languages. Again, while it is perfectly possible to devise a vocabulary for writing papers in molecular biology in Estonian, and for all I know this has been done, nobody who wishes to be read (except by the other Estonian molecular biologists) will write such papers. They will need to write them in internationally current languages, as even the French and the Germans have to do in such fields as economics. Only if the number of students coming into higher education is so large, and they are recruited from monoglot families, is there a sound educational reason for a full, vernacular, scientific vocabulary—and then only for introductory textbooks. For all more advanced purposes students will have to learn enough of an international language to read the literature, and probably also they will have to learn enough of the kind of English which is today, for intellectuals, what Latin was in the Middle Ages. It would be realistic today to give all university education in certain subjects in English, as is partly done in countries like the Netherlands and Finland which once were the pioneers of turning local vernaculars into all-purpose languages. There is no other way. Officially, nineteenth-century Hungary succeeded in making Magyar into such an all-purpose language for everything from poetry to nuclear physics. In practice, since only 10 million out of the world's 6,000 million speak it, every educated Hungarian has to be, and is, plurilingual.

What we have today is not interchangeable but complementary languages, whatever the official position. In Switzerland there is no pressure to turn Schwyzerdütsch into a written language, because there is no political objection to using High German, English and French for this purpose. (In Cataluña the cost of turning Catalan into an all-purpose language is to deprive the poor and uneducated inhabitants of this bilingual region of the native advantage of speaking and writing one of the few major international languages, namely Spanish.) In Paraguay everybody speaks Guaraní (well, strictly speaking 45 per cent of the population are bilingual), the Indian language which has, ever since the country was established as a Spanish colony, served as a regional lingua franca. However, though it has long had equal rights, so far as I can see it is used chiefly for writing poetry, theatre and similar purposes, and for other written purposes Spanish is used. It is extremely unlikely that in Peru, where Quechua (rightly) acquired official standing in the 1970s, there will be much demand either for daily newspapers or university education in that language. Why should there be? Even in Barcelona, where Catalan is universally spoken by the locals, in the mid-1990s the great majority of daily papers, including the Catalan edition of national papers, were in Spanish. As for the typical Third World state, as I have pointed out, it cannot possibly have just one all-purpose language.

This is the situation which has encouraged the rise of a lingua franca in countries and regions, and of English as a world-wide medium of communication. Such pidgins or creoles may be culture and literary languages, but that is not their main purpose. Medieval clerk's Latin had very little to do with Virgil and Cicero. They may or may not become official languages—for countries do need languages of general public communication—but when they are, they should avoid becoming monopoly culture languages. And the less we let the poets get their hands on such communication languages, the better, for poetry encourages both incommunicability and linguistic nationalism. On the other hand, such languages are tempted to let themselves be dominated by bureaucratic or technical jargon, since this is what they are primarily used for. This also should be fought in the interests of clarity. Since American English is already one of the most jargon-ridden idioms ever invented, the danger is real.

Let me conclude with some remarks about what one might call purely political languages—namely, languages which are created specifically as symbols of nationalist or regionalist aspiration, generally for separatist or secessionist purposes. The case for these is non-existent. The extreme example is the attempted reconstitution of the Cornish language, last spoken in the mid-eighteenth century, which has no other purpose than to demarcate Cornwall from England. Such constructed languages may succeed, like Hebrew in Israel (they may turn into real, spoken and living

languages) or they may fail, like the attempt by nationalist poets between the wars to turn the Scots dialect into a literary language
('Lallans'), but neither communication nor culture is the object of
such exercises. These are extreme cases, but all languages have
elements of such political self-assertion, for in an era of national or
regional secessionism there is a natural tendency to complement
political independence by linguistic separatism. We can see this
happening in Croatia at the moment. It has the additional advantage of providing a privileged zone of employment for a body of
nationalist or regionalist militants, as in Wales. Let me repeat once
again: politics and not culture is at the core of this language
manipulation, as the experts in the study of language purism have
established.[8] Czech language purism was directed mainly at the
elimination of German elements, but did not resist the mass influx
of French borrowings or the old Latin loan-words. This is natural
enough. The Ruthenes don't define themselves as a 'nation' with a
'language' in general, but specifically against the Ukrainians.[9]
Catalan nationalism is directed exclusively against Spain, just as
linguistic Welsh nationalism is directed exclusively against English.

However, there is today a new element encouraging the political
creation of languages, namely the systematic regionalization of
states. Regions without special linguistic, ethnic or other characteristics are joined, to potentially separatist areas, for example Murcia
to Catalonia. If Spain is a guide, this will lead eventually no doubt to
the creation of localized 'official' languages demanding monopoly
status, as in Cataluña. What is true of Valencia today may be true of
Picardy tomorrow.

This raises the spectre of general Balkanization. Given the European Union's policy of favouring regions against existing nation-
states, which is, *de facto*, a policy favouring separatism, as the Scots
and Catalan nationalists have quickly recognized, this is a real
problem. Balkanization will not solve any problems of linguistic
and cultural identity. We shall continue as before. Brussels may
spend one third of its income on translation and interpretation,
and if Europe can afford it, why not? But the affairs of the European
Union will not be primarily, or at all, conducted in Portuguese or

Greek, or even Danish and Dutch. What linguistic Balkanization will do is to multiply the occasions for conflict. If the Croats can create a separate language for themselves out of the unified Serbocroat which their forefathers constructed to unify the southern Slavs, then anybody can. So long as language is not as firmly separated from the state as religion was in the United States under the American constitution, it will be a constant and generally artificial source of civil strife.

Let us remember the Tower of Babel. It remained forever un-completed because God condemned the human race to everlasting linguistic conflict.

The Superiority of Collective Action: The Case of the NHS

DOROTHY WEDDERBURN

26 July 1945 saw the landslide victory of the Labour Party in the first post Second World War election. In three years, 1945–48, five pieces of legislation were enacted which together laid the foundation of the welfare state. The inspiration and context for this programme had been provided in 1943 by the Beveridge Report. Beveridge, himself a Liberal, had captured public imagination with his picture of five giants which had to be slain if a better world was to be created. These were the giants of want, disease, ignorance, squalor and idleness. The Attlee government legislation was directed at these giants and aimed to protect against the natural contingencies of life, old age, sickness and unemployment; to provide children's allowances; to make provision for education; and to ensure an adequate supply of housing. The 'superiority of collective action', as Aneurin Bevan called it, was taken for granted as a basis for social policy. In these days of political disaffection it is salutary to be reminded of the excitement, the hopes, aspirations, and shared sense of purpose among so many, which shaped the political scene. T. H. Marshall had no inhibitions about declaring in 1949, 'our modern system is frankly a socialist system, with the market functioning within limits'.[1]

This judgement was challenged at the time and since, but what Marshall certainly underestimated was the way in which the market would operate to weaken those limits and to generate new inequalities. The more closely the welfare-state provisions were modelled upon market arrangements, the more competition the market would eventually provide to the state system. Within a few years the growth in the coverage of occupational pensions, sick pay, and other fringe benefits provided by employers and linked to employment status (where far more middle-class than working-class occupations were covered) had turned state provision in these areas into a residual. At the same time the widespread sense of community which had informed support for the Labour government legislation began to weaken. By the 1960s different attitudes had emerged towards different aspects of welfare provision. Support for increases in old age pensions remained strong. Far less popular were unemployment and child benefits. Echoes of the Victorian distinction between the deserving and undeserving poor could be heard. And then in the 1970s the end of full employment produced such pressure upon the state benefit system that the questioning of the function of the welfare state, and the gradual erosion of its provisions which had already started, turned into an avalanche with the return of the Thatcher government in 1979. There was now explicit commitment to roll back the frontiers of the state; the values of collective action were rejected and the virtues of individualism and self-help were extolled.

There was one exception, however, namely the National Health Service. Even today, after the introduction in 1991 of the so called internal market in health care, which will be discussed later, the guiding principles of the NHS remain, at least nominally, those of its founding architect: Aneurin Bevan. These are a universal, comprehensive service, free at the point of delivery and—very important to Bevan—of the best available quality. How can we account for this continuity, almost as amazing as its original conception?

During the war a large measure of agreement had emerged between many diverse groups that measures were needed to deal with the manifest inadequacies and inequalities in access to medical treatment which characterized pre-war Britain. The only group which had access to free health care were employees earning less than £250 a year who paid health insurance contributions, and then they were only entitled to it for themselves: their families were not covered. In 1926 the Royal Commission on National Health

Insurance had already remarked: 'the ultimate solution will be, we think, in the direction of divorcing the medical service entirely from the insurance system and recognising it, along with all other public health activities, as a service to be supported from public funds'.

They merely commented. They made no recommendation to this effect. Various small-scale, voluntary contributory schemes grew up to cover working-class people including their families. But millions, not just working class, had difficulty with, or simply could not afford to pay for the care they needed from general practitioners or from hospitals. The quality of care was also problematic. It ranged from the good to the frankly bad. The geographical distribution was wholly illogical in terms of meeting need. In the 1930s even the British Medical Association was moved to produce proposals for a 'general medical service for the nation' and the Socialist Medical Association, not without influence within the Labour Party, began campaigning for a 'socialised medical service'. There was no shortage of debate, but it was the needs of the war itself which provided the spur to action, and subsequently to the production of plans for the future.[2] The wartime coalition government published a White Paper in 1944 introducing the concept of a comprehensive medical service for some 90 per cent of the population. Negotiations, particularly with the medical profession, were under way when the election took place. Thus, when Aneurin Bevan became Minister of Health in 1945 the major issues which had to be covered by the legislation were clear, and some of the opposition sticking points had been identified. But the radical character of the National Health Service Act, as passed in 1946, owes everything to Bevan's own commitment and vision, as well as to his skill as a negotiator. His vision, as described by his biographer Michael Foot, was to reach out for the ideal of a classless society.[3] Provision of health care was one step on that road. Bevan himself declared, with passion,

> No society can legitimately call itself civilised if a sick person is denied medical aid because of lack of means. Society becomes more wholesome, more serene, and spiritually healthier if it knows its citizens have at the back of their consciousness the knowledge that

not only themselves but all their fellows have access to the best that medical skill can provide.

The publication of Bevan's bill produced a violently hostile reaction among both the Conservatives in Parliament and large sections of the medical profession. Michael Foot's biography reproduces a Low cartoon with Bevan lying on an operating table with an army of gleeful doctors dismembering him and an even more gleeful Charles Hill, secretary of the BMA, saying, 'all that remains gentlemen is to remove the neck and the operation will be completely successful'.

Foot also provides a riveting account of the negotiation between the minister and the various sections of the medical establishment, and one cannot but be impressed by Bevan's single-mindedness and confidence in the face of professional opposition. Some important concessions were made, but the essentials of Bevan's objectives were met in the 1946 Act.

The key features of the legislation were: first, the NHS would be financed out of general taxation; the principle of insurance was rejected. Time would show this to be an extremely important decision. A parallel was drawn with nineteenth-century public health measures, although these were provided by local authorities, whereas in the new NHS structure they did not figure. Second, all hospitals, both voluntary and local authority, were taken into public ownership to become a national hospital service, run by the Department of Health with regional and district tiers of administration. Clinicians were to be employed by the local health authorities although, in negotiation, they won the right to engage in a limited amount of private practice. Third, general practitioners, after the bitterest and most protracted negotiations of all, were guaranteed their status as independent contractors within the NHS. They extracted an undertaking from Bevan that a salaried service would be ruled out, and they were free to decide whether or not to join the NHS. Having joined they were subject to some control over the right to set up in practice where they chose, if the area was judged to be over-doctored. They also lost the right to buy and sell practices for which, in return, they received lump-sum compensation. Amazingly, after early threats to boycott the new service, 90 per cent of GPs had signed up by vesting day in 1948 and within a few months 97 per cent of the public had registered with the GP of their choice.

In an article in the *Independent on Sunday*, celebrating the fiftieth anniversary of the election of a Labour government in 1945, Neal Ascherson described finding a leaflet given to him when he left the forces in 1950. It contained the form to be used to register with a GP and a description of the new health service. He remarked upon the clarity and sureness of language of the introductory paragraph:

> It [the NHS] will provide you with all medical, dental and nursing care. Everyone, rich or poor, man, woman or child, can use it or any part of it. There are no charges except for a few special items. There are no insurance qualifications. But it is not a 'charity'. You are all paying for it, mainly as taxpayers and it will relieve your money worries in time of illness.

The language is, indeed, a long way from NHS-'speak' today.

The introduction of the health service went remarkably smoothly but some voices were raised in alarm at the cost. Allegations of extravagant use grew. The level of expenditure had, perhaps almost inevitably, been underestimated because there was little reliable information available. The pressure to economize was such that, only three years after inauguration, prescription charges were introduced to be closely followed by a charge for spectacles and teeth. There were bitter struggles within the Labour Cabinet, however, before this step was taken which eventually led to the departure of Bevan from the Ministry of Health. Charges had, nevertheless, come to stay, although they were not enough to stem the chorus of criticism from those who alleged that the country could not afford the NHS. In 1953 a Conservative government established the Guillebaud Committee to 'consider how rising charges on the Exchequer might be avoided'. The committee took three years to report and when it did it offered no comfort to those who wished to reduce spending, for it gave a clean bill of health to the service. Indeed, it concluded by warning that, far from there being a possibility of economies, higher expenditure was likely to be required in the future as unmet need was uncovered, as public standards of adequacy rose and because of the need to rectify existing deficiencies, most notably in capital provision. Richard Titmuss and Brian Abel-Smith, from the London School of Economics, acted as consultants to the committee. In what was, for that time, a statistical innovation, now commonplace, they looked at the level of expenditure on the health service as a percentage of national income. To everyone's surprise, they found that, between 1949/50 and 1953/54, it had declined from 3.75 per cent to 3.24 per cent. Moreover, capital spending was at a lower level, in real terms, than before the war.[4]

None the less, the issue of cost was to remain central to government concerns and to public discussion about the health service. Yet no government, Conservative or Labour, felt bold enough to mount an attack upon its fundamental principles. Election manifestos of all sides declared a commitment to maintaining a free and universal service. A consensus on this issue had been arrived at and it held over the next twenty-four years. Actual spending on health care, in the period 1955 to the late 1970s, increased as a percentage of gross domestic product fairly steadily, but not dramatically, to reach 6.0 per cent. Although the Labour Party saw itself as the natural defender of Bevan's creation, such was the electoral popularity of the NHS that there was only a slight tendency for spending to rise faster under Labour than under Conservative governments.[5]

Other issues began to occupy centre stage, most notably issues of structure. This was not surprising in view of the size and complexity of the organization that had been created. Already in the early 1950s the NHS employed, mostly as independent contractors, 20,000 general practitioners, 10,000 pharmacists, and 7,000 opticians. Within the hospital service there were 7,000 consultants, 150,000 nurses, 150,000 domestic staff as well as technicians, radiographers, physiotherapists, and so on. Moreover the services provided were extremely diverse. In the direct provision of health care, procedures could range from the treatment of bunions to major surgery. The

NHS also made its contribution to research in medicine and the training of new entrants to the professions. It provided hotel services for those admitted to hospital and an ambulance service for transportation. The task of devising *appropriate* organizational structures to handle such complexity was a difficult one.

Four main organizational tensions run throughout the period to 1979. The first was between centralization and decentralization. The NHS became the direct statutory responsibility of a minister of the Crown, with a health department staffed by civil servants, and answerable to Parliament. The day-to-day management was devolved to health authorities, regional and local, (called variously district or area), who employed staff and provided both drugs and facilities and ensured the delivery of health services. There was clearly a gap between the formal responsibility of the minister and the operational reality, which caused difficulties. Altogether separate from this were the general practitioners and other independent contractors with their executive committees (renamed Family Practitioners Committees in 1974) responsible for contracts and terms of service and dealing directly with the department on these matters. At the centre, planning, implementation and monitoring were all combined in a unitary system which was never well-served with information. There was constant pressure for more devolution.

The second source of tension was between the professionals—the doctors—and the administrators or managers. For a long time the professionals were dominant. In the 1960s some commentators characterized the hospital consultants as themselves behaving like independent contractors, using the facilities provided by their hospital, but in no way involved in its overall functioning. Indeed, consultants used beds and operating theatres as their private property and took little notice of the impact of their decisions upon the most efficient use of resources. But gradually challenges to this professional dominance grew.

The third source of tension was related to the first two and raised the issue of accountability not only to Parliament for the expenditure of public money with probity, and for the implementation of overall policy, but also accountability for meeting the health-care needs of specific communities and individuals within them, which was, after all, the *raison d'être* for the service. In 1948 there was little recognition of this as a problem. Bevan had, initially, seemed prepared to contemplate a degree of industrial democracy within the structure he evolved, but not of local representation of 'consumers'. In the event, only the doctors were granted formal representation, and the remaining members of Regional Boards, District Health Authorities and Hospital Management Committees were all appointees. Not until 1975, under a Labour government, were local authorities given a formal voice on what were then newly introduced Area Health Authorities. Finally, there was the tension between what was to be regarded as 'health' and what was properly 'social services' and the responsibility of local authorities. All these tensions combined to give rise to periodic structural reorganizations, but it is the period since 1979, and more particularly since 1990 and the introduction of the 'internal market', which has witnessed the most profound changes.

The health service was not immune from social and economic change in the wider society. Scientific advances were beginning to have a profound effect upon the nature of medicine itself. Patients' expectations were rising and there were also changes in the attitudes and expectations of those who worked in the service, so that, in addition to the political sensitivities surrounding the cost of the service, were added problems of industrial relations. As we have seen the doctors were, from the beginning, well organized and vociferous but from the 1960s onwards other occupational groups became more vocal. This was a period of considerable growth in white collar trade unionism generally, but it was also the beginning of a series of government attempts at incomes policies to hold down the overall pressure of pay increases upon inflation. Public-sector employees were affected most directly. A series of major pay confrontations in the health service occurred in the 1970s, beginning with a strike of ancillary workers in 1973. In 1975 junior doctors withdrew their labour; and between 1974 and 1976 there was a long, running battle between the hospital consultants and Barbara Castle (then Labour's

Minister of Health) when she boldly attempted to end pay beds (the system whereby hospital consultants who undertook private practice could admit their patients to designated beds in NHS hospitals).

By the 1970s consumers were also finding a voice. The numbers of special-interest groups or lobbying organizations mushroomed and were actively orchestrating their demands on the NHS. In the 1974 Conservative reorganization Community Health Councils were set up as local watchdogs with powers, which they still possess, of seeking information and having the right to be consulted on proposed hospital closures or other major changes in service provision. This was a period of general turmoil in the NHS, and it was combined with a period of particularly acute pressure on resources. Yet another full-scale examination of the service seemed called for, and in 1976 Harold Wilson, in one of his last decisions as Labour Prime Minister, set up a Royal Commission which was requested, 'in the interests both of the patients and of those who work in the NHS, to recommend the best use and management of the financial and manpower resources of the NHS'.[6]

Once again the basic principles of the service were re-examined and once again it was found that there was no case to change them. The service was to remain financed directly by the Exchequer, and the principles of equality of entitlement and access and a service free at the point of use were reiterated. The general working of the NHS was given a clean bill of health. A substantial number of detailed and interesting recommendations were made mainly directed at addressing the tensions described above. In fact, however, the report was buried scarcely before it saw the light of day, because 1979 saw the election of Mrs Thatcher and a Conservative government which marks the beginning of a new era.

Many people expected a frontal assault upon the NHS in view of the ideological commitment of the new government to the private market and to a reduction in public expenditure. It did not come immediately despite the fact that the NHS was increasingly causing trouble. Public criticism of the service was mounting particularly because of long waiting lists, and militancy among the unions was growing. The initial response of the government was to place increased efficiency in the use of resources at the top of the agenda, and as one way of achieving this, to confront the professionals with a series of organizational changes. The Prime Minister was advised by Roy Griffiths, the managing director of Sainsbury at the time. His report served to transform the management style of the NHS from 'administration with consensus' to 'general management' as in commercial enterprises, with the object of placing the managers in the ascendance. At the top, strategic decision-making and the monitoring of implementation was increasingly separated from the carrying out of policy. New managers were appointed, at all levels, many from outside the NHS, and performance targets were introduced. Even the GPs had a new contract imposed upon them which contained elements of performance-related pay. It is worth noting, however, that government spending, which had fallen slightly under the previous Labour government, rose and continued to rise at 3 per cent per annum in real terms for the next thirteen years. Most surprising of all, however, was that the 1983 Conservative election manifesto declared that: 'The principles that adequate health care should be provided for all, regardless of ability to pay, must be a foundation of arrangements for financing health care.'

In the background other ideas were, however, being discussed. In the government's first term the Central Policy Review Group of the Cabinet Office produced an *internal* report which advocated privatization and the development of private health insurance. When the Prime Minister finally publicly announced her review of the NHS in 1988 this was, in fact, the initial option considered. But such was the political sensitivity of the issue that in quite a short time it was abandoned in favour of what has come to be known as the internal market. Kenneth Clarke, as Minister of Health, opted to retain a tax-financed NHS but to introduce competition. The measures were set out in the White Paper *Working for Patients* published in January 1989 which reiterated yet again: 'The principles which guided it [the NHS] for the last forty years will continue to guide it into the 21st Century. The NHS is and will continue to be open to all regardless of income and financed out of general taxation.'⁷ But there were huge organizational changes envisaged which involved separating the direct provision of health services from purchasing.

At the top, policy formation and operational responsibilities were firmly separated with the creation of an NHS Executive with its own board distinct from the Department of Health. Hospitals, community and mental-health services all became independent trusts governed by *appointed* boards of executive and non-executive members. They were required to generate enough income to balance their books and produce a 6 per cent return on capital employed. They were free to accept work from the private sector and were positively encouraged to use competitive tendering, or market testing, for services which they could subcontract, not only domestic or 'hotel' services but also clinical services. Providers would, however, have to attract work from 'purchasers'. There would be two types of public purchaser. District health authorities (composed again of executive and appointed non-executive members), would purchase to meet the health needs of their geographical population. Their budget would be allocated via the Regional Health Authority and it would be calculated on a weighted capitation formula to make some allowance for differences of need—for example, age structure, and degree of deprivation. The second kind of purchaser introduced quite a new concept. GPs (initially with a list size over 9,000, although that number was soon reduced) could elect to become 'fund-holders'. They would receive a budget transferred from the resource allocated to their District Health Authority to enable them to purchase, directly from trusts, drugs, diagnostic hospital services and non-emergency hospital and community care for their patients. The thinking behind this structure was that providers would be competing for contracts from purchasers and would thus be encouraged to be more efficient in order to reduce their prices, and also be forced to pay more attention to what purchasers indicated that their patients wanted. Purchasers would be close to their patients and would be able to translate their needs into the requirements of contracts responsive to those needs. They would also seek to maximize the amount of health care which they could buy by seeking out providers who would supply at the lowest price.

The new structures were rapidly adopted. The first hospital trusts were established in 1991 and, by 1995, 90 per cent of the population was served by 450 trusts. GP fund-holding spread rapidly, although unevenly in different parts of the country. By 1995 more than 50 per cent of the population was registered with GP fund-holders, and the growth has continued. The overall structure of the NHS has also continued to evolve with two important further changes. In April 1996, Regional Health Authorities were abolished and replaced by small regional offices of the NHS Executive, and District Health Authorities were merged with Family Health Service Authorities (the name which the bodies responsible for the administration of family practitioner services had acquired) to create unified Health Authorities coterminous with the relevant local authorities. Since the beginning of 1996 the main line of accountability for the operation of the service has run from the NHS Executive and its board to individual health authorities.

Such, however, are the inadequacies of health-service statistics (getting worse as the centralized system is dismantled) that it is impossible to sum up satisfactorily the consequences of the internal market to date. The government claimed more patients treated, improvements in the process involved in actually obtaining treatment (for example, shorter waiting times) and imaginative innovations in the delivery of care to the benefit of patients. Some of that is true. Critics, on the other hand, point to the fact that GPs, particularly in London, have had great difficulty in finding beds; that operations are frequently cancelled at the last moment; and that waiting times are still unacceptably long both for hospital treatment and for appointments with GPs. Accident and Emergency departments have been closed for lack of qualified staff, in addition to those that have been closed as part of programmes of rationalization. There is *prima-facie* evidence that both hospitals and GPs are working under increasing pressure, both because of inadequate staffing and because of an increase in morbidity. As for fund-holding, it is widely believed to have given rise to a two-tier system, where patients of fund-holders receive superior and preferential treatment in secondary care, particularly for non-emergency acute conditions. It is also asserted that it has encouraged the fragmentation of non-hospital clinical services, providing opportunities for the private sector to step in with no guarantee of value for money. There is no satisfactory mechanism in place for assessing the overall quality of the decisions that GP fund-holders make, nor for evaluating the long-term consequences for the care provided for certain vulnerable groups in the new system. It is widely feared, for example, that mental-health patients may suffer. To the extent that GP fund-holding spreads and more of the population become covered the two-tier objection will weaken. But there have always, unfortunately, been variations in the treatment of patients between different GPs which reflect basic differences in competence, diligence and knowledge. It is well known that there are wide variations in prescribing and referral patterns. Fund-holding could exacerbate these differences. Whether it does or not, however, a major concern is the additional difficulty it will create for the essential task of co-ordination and planning of the service, and the additional administrative costs which fund-holding itself imposes.

In fact the use of contracting has resulted inevitably in a substantial increase in administrative costs for both purchasers and providers. Public criticism has mounted and the NHS Executive is now attempting to contain it. The abolition of regions was one step. Another is the cap which has been placed upon the management costs of so-called independent trusts and health authorities alike. As for major structural change in the configuration of services or in the structure of trusts, the internal market has shown itself, not surprisingly, incapable of delivering the necessary adjustments. Some Outer London health authorities have moved contracts from Inner London to cheaper suppliers in the periphery and this has caused some discomfort. But the major influence upon the restructuring of hospitals in Inner London has remained the direct action of the Department of Health to protect some trusts in the face of 'market' pressures and to force others to merge or close. Parallel interventions to rationalize the provision of certain specialties both in London and elsewhere are also being led centrally. The centre–periphery tension which was noted earlier as a continuing characteristic of the NHS organization in the first thirty years of its life has not gone away.

In the absence of clear evidence, response to the internal market so far has been coloured by political viewpoint. One most unfortunate consequence has been that the management of the service has been drawn into defending the policy of the government on the basis of highly dubious 'statistics'. An atmosphere of mistrust has grown among the public and the professional–managerial tension has intensified. At its strongest, this mistrust gave rise to the widespread belief that the changes really represented the first step towards the privatization of the health service as and when the Conservative government judged the moment to be ripe: a softly, softly approach. So far, however, whatever the intention, the political popularity of the NHS is still sufficient to have put a brake upon any such objective and the incursions of private finance and activity have been confined to the margins. The current political climate appears such that it might not be too late for any future Labour government, as Neal Ascherson has put it, 'to burn the worst market absurdities out of the NHS'.

The Labour Party stands firmly in defence of a health service financed from taxation, but seems to accept that there will be no return to the organizational *status quo* as it was before 1991. Trusts will stay, but they will be subject to more co-ordination and control. Contracts might go, and be replaced by a rolling programme of service-level agreements. GP fund-holding will be transformed by a system of joint commissioning between District Health Authorities and GPs, examples of which are developing spontaneously in some areas. Sadly, however, on the thorny question of additional resource for the NHS the need for which is now overwhelming, the Labour Party has been evasive. There is lack of clarity about the mechanisms which might be needed both to articulate and implement policy over the next ten years, and in particular to deal with the organizational tensions which have characterized the service, long before the internal market was thought of. The crude market mechanism has been shown not to work but neither will the mishmash which has emerged from the 1991 changes, particularly in the face of the extremely complex issues which surround the provision of health care into the next century. It is to some of those issues that we must now turn.

First, it is relevant to consider whether history has justified Bevan's belief in the 'superiority of collective action'. The answer, in my view, is still clearly 'yes'. To date there is no obvious sign of a rush of those who can afford private health care to opt out of the NHS. The numbers of people with private health insurance have, it is true, increased since the mid-1970s. Employers (and even some trade unions) began to offer private insurance as yet another fringe benefit, and the Conservative government's tax concession on health insurance premiums for pensioners provided an additional fillip. But it seems that the users of the private sector have been seeking to satisfy demands that are not primarily *medical* in character. Rather they have sought to improve aspects of the *delivery* of health care, which the NHS at present frustrates—such matters as the preference for privacy, and above all to be treated at the time of, and by the consultant of, one's choice. Private health insurance has frequently been used as a supplement to NHS provision. The strength of competition from the private sector in the future seems likely still to turn upon the quality of the service which the NHS itself can offer.

There are, of course, many ways in which the NHS can be criticized, but on the criteria of equity and ease of access to health care it scores higher than most advanced industrialized countries. The United States provides the extreme contrast. With the highest percentage of national income of Western industrial countries spent on health care (14 per cent) it is estimated that, without reform (which now seems remote after the defeat of President Clinton's proposed health-care legislation of 1993), 25 per cent of all Americans will be without health insurance for some period over the next five years. Access to needed medical services is severely restricted for large numbers of citizens. At the same time such is the inefficiency of the existing system that the private hospital groups, which provide much of the health care, are able to make a profit with low levels of bed occupancy.

It has to be admitted that there are inequalities persisting within the National Health Service but they are not the result of 'collective provision', as such. They reflect, among other things, historical differences in resource allocation between regions, and the nature of medicine including the differences of practice between individual doctors, referred to earlier. More worrying, because not well understood, are the variations in outcomes in terms of mortality and morbidity for different groups of the population, which are associated with characteristics such as gender, ethnic group and socio-economic status. This phenomenon is to be observed in most countries whatever the basis of their health-care systems. In the United Kingdom, however, renewed interest in understanding the causes of such differences was stimulated by the publication of the Black Report in 1980 which suggested that they might actually be increasing.[8] The Department of Health eventually established a working group to examine what steps should be taken to reduce health variations, observing that they 'indicate the extent of potential preventable ill-health and premature death'.

It reported at the end of 1995.[9] The conclusions were disappointing, perhaps because inequalities in health care are inextricably intertwined with other social inequalities which the Department of Health alone cannot address. I return to this problem later. To the extent that any message emerged it was that effective action requires inter-agency collaboration, the targeting of resources and the adoption of a time-scale for change which only a comprehensive national health system could provide.

The NHS has also proved itself superior to other systems, for the delivery of health care, in other ways. The administrative costs of British health care were some of the lowest in the world and despite the introduction of the internal market remain so. Moreover the direct medical costs of provision are also extremely low. Various reasons account for this. First the method of paying NHS doctors has not provided any incentive to 'induce' demand. Another reason was the concession wrung from Aneurin Bevan to grant doctors in primary care independence from the hospital service. Paid largely by capitation, GPs facilitate access to medical care by their closeness to the patient but also, by acting as gatekeepers for more expensive secondary care, serve to keep down costs. Finally collective provision has put the NHS into the position of being a monopoly buyer of doctors' services and therefore able to contain doctors' remuneration.

As for the quality of the *medical* content of care in the NHS, it is more difficult to assess. Attempts to correlate statistics of mortality and morbidity with numbers of trained health-care personnel across countries are inconclusive. The quality of medical education in this country is regarded as superior to that of many other systems (at least, it is said, medical students actually get to see patients) and there is still evidence of innovation and medical advance which is impressive.

For reasons already considered, appeal to the *level* of spend expressed as a percentage of national income does not help us greatly in our search for an answer to questions about quality. However, it supports the view that a collectivist solution is not a costly one. We have already seen in the United States an example where high spend can still leave huge lacunae. On the other hand it may now be significant that Britain's percentage spend at 6.6 per cent of GNP in 1991 was one of the lowest in Europe along with Portugal, Denmark, Spain and Greece: all, with the exception of Denmark, among the poorer countries of Europe. So do we need to take another critical look at the present adequacy of the spend on health care in Britain?

There are certainly signs of growing strains in the NHS which are arising not just because of the latest reorganization, and its associated administrative costs, but because of increasing demands which have not yet been sufficiently acknowledged. The impact of the ageing population is one. Age-related needs expanded almost as rapidly over the 1980s as the volume of NHS resources.[10] Although the proportion of the population over 65 will not increase in the future as rapidly as in some other industrialized countries, the number of the very old (over 85) will certainly make greater demands for health care. The population is also becoming more heterogeneous in other ways. The medical needs of immigrants and refugees are both great, and different in many respects from the indigenous population. The increase in the number of single-person households may be responsible for the growth in demand for night home visits from GPs and for emergency hospital admissions which are on the increase in every locality. New problems like the asthma epidemic have emerged, while old diseases which it was thought had been conquered, TB for example, are re-emerging. We do not know what lies in store for us in terms of hitherto unidentified diseases like AIDS. Finally the impact of unemployment, redundancy and general social unease has, I believe, contributed to increased morbidity. These considerations all suggest that there are pressing reasons to increase the UK spend on health care. But there are none which suggest that a collectivist approach will be anything other than the most effective way of doing it.

Is public opinion, which has so far supported the collectivist solution, changing? Will it be powerful enough, in the face of pressures to contain public expenditure, to ensure that the government responds to the need for more resources? The decision, in 1946, to finance the service out of general taxation rather than through insurance has proved to be a crucial one. Not only did it guarantee access to health care for all but it has also facilitated control over costs by the government. Are these objectives becoming incompatible? By taking decisions at the centre about how much resource in total should be devoted to health care, pressures to increase spending are played out in the political arena where, in theory, the electorate are collectively involved. Even Mrs Thatcher understood this. She may also have understood that the purchaser–provider split could, to some extent, deflect any criticism about the adequacy of resource from central government to the local level because, it could be said, that is now where decisions about the use of resources will be taken. The evidence we have about public attitudes, for example, from the British Social Attitudes Survey, suggests not only a growing level of support, but a willingness to pay higher taxes for the NHS.[11] But why has public support for Bevan's basic principles been so strong and persistent? There is clearly something special about health which marks it out in the public mind from other desirable goods. Life, death and suffering have great resonances for us all, and we are all aware, to a greater or lesser degree, that we are each individually at risk. Moreover ill health still touches cords of sympathy for others. But there is an additional factor. Until very recently medical need appeared capable of *objective* definition and, what is more, definition by the professional, the doctor, the expert. This is in contrast to the definition of other welfare needs. Take, for example, the definition of a minimum income, about which there can be much debate and which contains a large component of relativity. This objective characteristic of absolute need in the context of health helped to create a widespread presumption in favour of using collective provision. The national health service therefore succeeded in retaining the support of the middle classes.

But is this situation changing? There are two relevant factors here. First, as medical technology advances, the 'need' for health care in terms of what is technically possible becomes more problematic. There is no simple life or death criterion. Secondly, as we see the room for difference of opinion about 'need' expand, so too we see the role of the professional as the arbiter of need increasingly challenged by the manager as the arbiter of cost. The conflict between the 'possible' and the 'affordable' is now central to all health-care systems, including Britain's, and public opinion has a less simple touchstone to guide it in its support of the principle of 'free health care to all who need it'. We may therefore ask: is the advance of medical technology creating a situation where a collectivist solution is no longer possible? All health services in the developed world are confronting this dilemma. There are new drugs, new equipment, new processes requiring more highly trained personnel, all of which establish new ways of tackling old problems, as well as the possibility of tackling conditions which could not be dealt with before but which all increase expenditure. The advance has created the nightmare where some find it possible to assert that the demand for health care *could* be infinite. This is clearly nonsense, but coming on top of the known pressures of increased demand such as the ageing of the population it poses a major problem.

Here we encounter the pressures of the private sector, not in the form of direct competition in provision, but in shaping what can be on offer. Many of the basic knowledge advances which have made these technological developments possible have originated in the health service itself as a result of research. Development and exploitation, however, for the most part lie with private-sector companies, operating and competing world-wide for profit, and without regard to the priorities which might be accorded by a national judgement of areas of greatest need. Even in drug development, where some national systems of control exist, they are primarily concerned with safety and not with an evaluation of the relative effectiveness of new drugs or of their importance for a system of national priorities. As for medical procedures, systems of evaluation are primitive, not only of new ones but also of existing ones which are often recognized to be of doubtful value. Much of the drive for adoption of the 'new' comes from the physicians themselves motivated by such diverse considerations as proving their skill and winning recognition as well as serving their patients. But this is also an area where the external-market system impinges directly upon the public system, because the physicians are under pressure, and sometimes extreme pressure, to use the products of the private system. This is seen most clearly with the pharmaceutical companies. A comprehensive but independent method of systematic evaluation is essential if costs are to be contained. There can be no doubt that collective provision, in the shape of a national health service, is best placed to embark upon such an undertaking, possibly as Brian Abel-Smith has suggested, through the European Union which has now been given a mandate to co-ordinate action in public health.[12] It will take a long time. Meanwhile the well-co-ordinated research and development activity which such an initiative requires will be more difficult to achieve in the UK if the present trend to fragmentation within the internal market is allowed to proceed further. It also requires political will on the part of government to use the bargaining power with drug and medical-technology companies which the existence of a national health-care system provides.

Given that the resource constraint is real, I suspect that we may well be faced with defining the set of core activities which a universal free service should provide. District Health Authorities have already begun to exclude certain procedures from their contracts, such as cosmetic surgery, or in-vitro fertilization. This poses a dilemma because defenders of the Bevan ideals fear that to concede that the health-care system today cannot provide *everything* that might be possible is the first step on the road to creating a two-tier service. In my view, however, to adopt this position is to open the door to creeping decisions without public debate and without adequate information. The experience of other countries which have attempted to deal with the problem should be studied closely with the principle of the defence of equity centre stage.

Finally there is the important question concerning the relationship of health care to other social provision. Over the life of the NHS lip service has been paid to the importance of prevention rather than cure and this has figured very prominently in the thinking of both the Conservative government and the Labour Party. Whilst the health service can make its contribution to prevention (perhaps people listen more if their doctor tells them to stop smoking than if they are exposed to a general campaign), I believe the main task of the service is what has been termed 'curing and caring'. The health service is so often picking up the consequence of failings of economic and social policy in other areas such as unemployment, poverty, inadequate housing and, increasingly today, preventable health risks created by environmental hazards. No government, Labour or Conservative, has made a serious attempt to unravel the interconnections between the various policies or even begun to develop a framework for resource allocation which could encompass and influence them.

There is, in any case, a difficulty with gaining public support for a policy which might advocate the spending of more money on housing, say, as a more effective way to improve health status than directly on curing illness. The particular appeal of the collective provision of health care lies in the immediacy of the consequences of health for most individuals. This is not the case with other forms of social provision where the lead time for demonstrating health improvements is longer. But we are unlikely to be able to ignore these possible trade-offs in the future for they are becoming ever more pressing. Inequality of economic condition in this country has grown alarmingly over the last fifteen years. In February 1995 the Rowntree Foundation published the results of their Commission of Inquiry into Income and Wealth.[13] Four of their main findings were:

- Income inequality in the UK grew rapidly between 1977 and 1990 reaching a higher level than has been recorded *since before the war*.

- Until 1980 wealth inequalities narrowed, but have now levelled out and despite the levelling are still very great.

- Income inequality has grown in a number of industrial countries but not all, and in the UK it has increased both to a greater extent and more rapidly than elsewhere.

- Over the period the poorest 20–30 per cent of the population have failed to share in economic growth, in contrast to the experience in the rest of the post-war period.

Whether or not these trends will continue depends, in part, on world economic conditions but more directly upon political choices, and purposive government action.

There is a school of thought which argues that the degree of inequality in itself, irrespective of the absolute levels of material standards, contributes to morbidity.[14] It is argued that perceptions of inequality by those who are *relatively* deprived translate into feelings of lack of security, lower self-esteem, even envy and misery which in turn influence health. Whether it is the psychological conditions themselves producing stress-related illness, or whether it is that these conditions lead to unhealthy life-styles, remains to be investigated. Be that as it may, the demands on the health service which stem from the general deterioration visible across the social fabric of this country today are already mounting. We need, not just a comprehensive health service, but a comprehensive and integrated social policy. This is what Bevan thought that he was beginning to shape in 1945.

His vision caught the imagination and the mood of the general public. We seem to be a long way from that mood today, but there is some reason for optimism. There are small signs of a reaction against extreme individualism and the inevitable inequalities remorselessly generated by an unfettered market. To translate vision into political action, however, requires both the clear articulation of policy, and honesty about the costs.

Promise and Performance: Why We Need an Official Poverty Report

A. B. ATKINSON

The main news item on 1 April 2001 was:

- At midday today, the Director of the Office for National Statistics published this year's *Poverty Report*, showing that the government had failed to meet its poverty target for the second successive year.

- The Prime Minister subsequently made a statement in the House of Commons announcing his intention to ask the monarch for Parliament to be dissolved.

- Labour failed to meet its promised performance standard despite having set itself only the target of preventing an increase in the poverty rate, in contrast to the Conservatives' election promise of reducing poverty through increased selectivity of social security benefits.

Such a situation scarcely seemed credible back in 1996. First, it seemed incredible that poverty would feature so largely in British politics. Is this not Old Labour? Or Beveridge or Lloyd George? Second, it seemed incredible that a government would stand or fall on the basis of its election promises. Conservative governments of the 1980s and 1990s may have encouraged the use of performance-related pay; they may have introduced citizen's charters and targets for privatized utilities. But it would be quite a different matter to apply performance standards to the government's own achievements. It must have been a divided House of Commons which passed the amendment of electoral law which required a government to resign if it failed to meet its election promises.

I will not in fact ask you to suspend disbelief to the extent of supposing that the government would agree to an electoral term which depends on its performance ('three misses and they are out'). It will be allowed to continue to believe that what is sauce for the goose is not necessarily sauce for the gander. But I am going to ask you to accept for the course of this essay that poverty in the United Kingdom[1] is a legitimate concern of citizens, and I am going to make the case for the adoption of a national performance target. The UK would have for the first time an official poverty line, decoupled from social security benefit rates. Reducing poverty would become an object of policy, and the Office for National Statistics would be requested to produce an annual *Poverty Report* assessing how far the target in the UK had been reached. Just like the *Inflation Report* of the Bank of England, the aim of this report would be 'to produce a wholly objective and comprehensive analysis'.[2] Each year, we would be able to see how far performance matched promise.

Decoupling poverty standards and benefit scales: experience in the UK, the EU, and the United States

The fact that the UK does not have an official poverty line may appear remarkable in view of the pioneering contributions of British social scientists to the study of poverty and of the predominance of poverty among the concerns that led to its social security system with largely flat-rate benefit scales. It is, however, the ambiguous relation between the two—that is, poverty standards and benefit rates—which may account for the failure to adopt a transparent national target.

The ambiguity was evident in the Beveridge Plan of 1942.

Beveridge stated that 'social insurance should aim at guaranteeing the minimum income needed for subsistence',[3] and presented his proposed benefit scales as achieving that objective. But subsistence was not the only consideration influencing the determination of benefit scales. According to John Veit Wilson, on the basis of his research on the Beveridge Committee papers, 'the driving forces were the need ... to keep costs largely within what could be taxed by horizontal redistribution by national insurance within the working class, and not to set scales which, it was believed, would remove the incentives to earn.'[4] For all that Beveridge may have given the opposite impression, he faced the dilemma of balancing social commitments and financial prudence, which is the subject of the essay in this volume by Amartya Sen.

In any case, the postwar legislation setting in place a national minimum rejected Beveridge's recommendation that the minimum should be guaranteed by social insurance. Instead it was National Assistance, the means-tested scheme, which played this role. And it was to National Assistance that social investigators in the postwar period looked when seeking a standard to judge the effectiveness of the welfare state. In *The Poor and the Poorest*, Brian Abel-Smith and Peter Townsend took the National Assistance scale as their starting-point, and later authors, including myself, followed their lead in using as a 'performance standard' the level of National Assistance, by then re-named Supplementary Benefit, and now called Income Support.[5]

There was no official poverty line, and the defects of the Income Support scale were evident. As reiterated by successive government spokesmen, both Labour and Conservative, any improvement in Income Support would, on this basis, lead to an *increase* in the number of people living at or below the poverty line. The position was made quite clear by Mrs Thatcher in July 1983, when she said at Prime Minister's Questions that 'there is no definition of the poverty line—[Hon Members: 'Oh.']—and there never has been under any Government'.[6] In 1989 the Secretary of State for Social Security, John Moore, went further and attacked the whole idea that there might be poverty in the UK. In a speech called 'The End of the Line for Poverty', he argued that poverty had been abolished, and that it therefore made no sense to use the word.

The Conservative government has been particularly concerned to attack the notion of poverty adopted by the European Union. Whereas the British government has no official poverty line, the European Commission has established such a criterion, stating that 'the poor shall be taken to mean persons, families and groups of persons whose resources (material, cultural and social) are so limited as to exclude them from the minimum acceptable way of life in the Member States in which they live'.[7] This is the definition contained in a decision of the Council of Ministers when approving the first Community Action Programme to Combat Poverty. In its evaluation of the programme, the Commission took as the concrete implementation of this definition a poverty standard of 50 per cent of the average disposable income per equivalent adult in the country in question. A poverty threshold of 50 per cent of the average is used in Eurostat publications.

There can, therefore, be said to be an official European Union poverty line. And there are other countries which have official lines, notably the United States. In 1964, when the War on Poverty was declared by President Johnson, the Council of Economic Advisers defined the poverty line as $3,000 a year for a family and $1,500 for a single person. This was based on research by Mollie Orshansky, who subsequently produced a refined, more differentiated, poverty line. This latter line was adopted in May 1965 by the Office of Economic Opportunity as 'a working definition of poverty for statistical, planning and budget purposes'.[8] In August 1969, the Bureau of the Budget issued a statistical policy directive which gave a modified version of the line official status throughout the Federal government.

Today, the US official poverty line is still in use, if modified in certain respects and adjusted over time. It is the basis for the Bureau of the Census Current Population Report, *Poverty in the United States*, which in 1992 showed that 14.5 per cent of the US population, or some 37 million people, were living in families with incomes below the poverty level. The mean poverty gap was $5,751 a year. Fifteen million people lived in families with incomes below *half* the official poverty line. The report contains a great deal of detail: 235 pages of text and tables. Poverty status is analysed by (among other variables) type of family, race, age, region, years of schooling, and work experience. The tables are accompanied by commentary: for example, in 1992 'the number of poor showed a statistically significant rise from the corresponding 1991 figure . . . This represents the third consecutive annual increase . . . Prior to 1990, the poverty rate had not increased since 1982'.[9]

The origins of the US official poverty line were not in social security benefit scales. Although the poverty line has played a role in the allocation of Federal funds and in the determination of individual benefits, the poverty line and the determination of benefits are essentially decoupled. There is no guarantee that the cash-transfer programmes will bring people up to the official poverty level. In January 1992, under the Aid to Families with Dependent Children programme, the maximum benefit, including food stamps, in the median state—since it varies by state—for a single parent family of three was only 72 per cent of the poverty threshold. For the elderly, the level of the Supplemental Security Income plus social security and food stamps was 86.2 per cent of the poverty threshold for a single person.[10]

An official *Poverty Report* for the UK?

Should the UK follow the example of the United States and adopt an official poverty line which is decoupled from benefit scales? Should we, indeed, go beyond this and interpret the poverty standard as a performance target? After all, this is not such an alien idea. The Major government was willing to set itself a specific target (2.5 per cent) for the rate of inflation.[11] Another government might set a target for unemployment. What is being suggested here is that we should look at poverty, too, when assessing economic performance.[12]

The parallel with inflation targets suggests, moreover, that we should follow the Bank of England's innovation of publishing the *Inflation Report*, and introduce a regular *Poverty Report* on the extent and nature of poverty.[13] The Office for National Statistics would be charged with publishing annually statistics on the UK population with incomes below specified percentages of the official poverty line, and their relation to the national performance target. The calculations in the *Poverty Report* would be the responsibility of the Director of the Office for National Statistics, who—like the Economics Department of the Bank of England—would apply and develop the appropriate professional standards. No doubt these would include an assessment of the uncertainty surrounding the estimates (as with the Bank's confidence intervals surrounding its inflation forecasts). A government would not fall simply on account of sampling error.[14]

The nucleus of such a report already exists in the form of the valuable publication *Households Below Average Income*, developed over the past ten years by the Analytical Services Division of the Department of Social Security.[15] If the official poverty line were to take the form of a percentage of mean income (and we were to accept certain other assumptions), as with the European Union poverty standard, then we already have much of the necessary material. The proportion of the population living in households with incomes below 40, 50 and 60 per cent of the mean income over the period 1979–1993/4 are shown in the graph.

The simple publication of statistics, however, is not enough. What is required is a statement of intent. The *Inflation Report* acquires its special significance on account of the government's inflation target. The reduction of poverty has to be an ambition of the government, just like the reduction of inflation. The figures in the *Poverty Report* have to be seen as indicating how far we are from achieving a national goal.

Essential to the proposal is that the official poverty scale should be set independently of social security benefit rates. It is important to keep these separate. The poverty target is an *objective*; social security benefits are an *instrument*. As it was put by John Veit

How many people are on low incomes?

%UK population living in households below different thresholds, defined relative to mean income

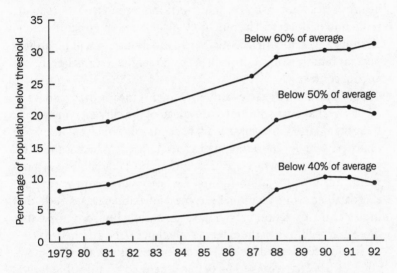

Source: Table F1 (before housing costs) in *Households Below Average Income* 1979–1992/93, 1979–1990/91, and 1979–1988/89.

Wilson in his case for a Minimum Income Standard (MIS), 'setting an MIS is one thing. It depends on social values and political aspirations for social justice. Setting income maintenance levels is another and different procedure affected by other considerations of politics and economics.'[16] It is for this reason that I propose that the *Poverty Report* should be the responsibility of the Office for National Statistics, rather than the Department of Social Security. The setting of national objectives should not be a matter for the public spending round.

The national performance standard, and the political commitment, would be set in terms of *outcomes* rather than social transfer policy instruments. The government would be committed not to raising child benefit by £X, or pensions by £Y, but to reducing poverty. The outcome will, of course, depend on the choice of benefit levels, but it will also depend on other policies. Macro-economic policy, employment policy, training programmes and health policies, for instance, may contribute as much or more to the reduction of poverty. The outcome will also depend on unforeseen circumstances, to which policies need to adjust. It will be an important function of the *Poverty Report* to set the national performance in context.

Separation of objectives and instruments means that we have to recognize that our aspirations run ahead of the current constraints. In terms of Jan Tinbergen's theory of economic policy, the abolition of poverty is a *flexible* rather than a *fixed* target.[17] Whereas the latter specifies policy objectives in absolute terms (the balance of payments must be in equilibrium or the borrowing requirement not exceed x per cent of national income), a flexible target is one that indicates the direction in which we are aiming but recognizes that there may be limits to the extent to which it can be attained.

The stance adopted by Western governments towards the alleviation of poverty seems to be better described as a flexible target. Governments recognize a social obligation, but its attainment is limited as a result of the constraints faced and the trade-off with other objectives. Beveridge may have claimed in his 1942 plan that the level of the subsistence standard determined the level of social insurance benefits, but in reality the choice of target was influenced by what was feasible. Behind his proposals lay a balancing of the benefit levels with considerations of cost and incentive constraints. In the present day, we may be setting an official poverty line which differs in both level and structure from the levels of National Insurance or Income Support.

What is more, the target set by the government may have a temporal dimension. No one can reasonably expect poverty to be ended overnight. For instance, the government may aim to ensure (a) that poverty does not rise and (b) that it is reduced by 5 percentage points by the end of the Parliament. In the USSR, when Khrushchev revived the calculation of minimum budgets, the government set a 'current' minimum, but also a 'prospective' minimum that looked to the future possibilities which it hoped expanding production would bring. It is too late for the UK to set the abolition of poverty as a target for the Millennium, but it may be a reasonable aspiration for 2015, when the children born today will become adults.

The adoption of such a performance standard may seem entirely natural. As Dr Johnson said, 'a decent provision for the poor is the true test of civilisation'. Even without the introduction of performance-related rewards for the government, a national poverty indicator would provide a focus for such a concern, and the *Poverty Report* would inform public debate. The press and media would find such a poverty standard simple to describe, and there would be clear topical interest in government performance according to this target. In the United States, newspapers know when the annual poverty count is to be released and line up academic commentators. The regular performance test would contribute to keeping the issue on the public agenda. In this connection, we should note the importance attributed by Jean Drèze and Amartya Sen to the role played by the press and media in the avoidance of famine in such countries as India.[18] Moreover, at the 1995 Copenhagen Summit on Social Development, the British government committed itself to a national plan to 'establish . . . strategies and affordable time-bound goals and targets for the substantial reduction of overall poverty and the eradication of absolute poverty'. The *Poverty Report* would indicate the progress made, and it would also be relevant to the Social Chapter of the European Union.

What, then, are the arguments against? The first set of arguments is that we could not agree on the definition of a poverty line and the contents of the *Poverty Report*. Academics disagree about fundamental conceptual issues; pressure groups disagree about their implementation. One can almost hear a government minister saying with scorn that he invited twenty-five representatives of the 'poverty lobby' to a meeting to decide on the poverty line and that he came out with twenty-five different views. The second and third sets of objections accept that we can define an official line but are sceptical about whether its adoption would contribute to the reduction of poverty. At worst, establishment of an official poverty line could be cathartic and have a negative impact on anti-poverty policy. It would be counter-productive. At best, sceptics hold that announcing such a target would be mere words, and would add nothing to the concrete policy initiatives taken. The final set of objections is raised by those who can see no reason why a government should agree to a performance target. Why should a political party give such a hostage to fortune? On the other hand, governments have in the past done so—as instanced by the 2.5 per cent inflation target, which provides a parallel which runs through this essay.

These, then, are the questions I want to consider in the rest of this essay:

- Could we agree on a poverty line and on the contents of a *Poverty Report*?
- Would a national poverty objective be counter-productive?
- Would a *Poverty Report* make any difference?
- Why should a government accept a performance target?

Could we agree on a poverty line?

For some people, inflation is not a problem; they do not see why its reduction should be a national goal. Others feel that hyper-inflation is a problem, but that it is not relevant to Britain. Latin American countries are the ones which need to worry about inflation. The same is true of poverty. Some people do not regard it as a problem. Others say that there is no poverty in the UK; they feel that there is no need for the UK government to introduce a poverty-eradication plan; this is a matter for 'underdeveloped' countries.

There is bound to be disagreement about national goals. Even among those who support the reduction of poverty, there is, as noted above, much disagreement about its definition. The academic literature is replete with discussions of the difficulties in defining a poverty line. From this literature, readers will recognize the problems with my earlier use of the European Union's 50 per cent poverty line. For some, the definition will already have closed too many options. It may not be adequate to measure poverty in terms of income, rather than expenditure or the consumption of specific commodities, such as food or shelter. Income may be an intermediate variable, rather than an end in itself, allowing people to achieve a certain level of functioning. For others, it will have left open too many questions. In work with Karin Gardiner, Valerie Lechêne and Holly Sutherland, I have shown how a '50 per cent of average income' criterion can be interpreted in very different ways, leading to quite different comparative rankings of different countries.[19] In countries where there are large regional differences, it may be asked whether it is appropriate to apply the national average, or whether there should be different, regional poverty lines.

All of this poses formidable problems, and it is far from clear that we could agree on a national target. At the same time, there are three considerations which make the task of agreement easier.

First, there is an important difference between agreeing on a criterion according to which benefits are to be paid and agreeing on a definition for purely statistical purposes. We do not have to worry about the feasibility of the administrative apparatus for determining benefit eligibility. If it is an aggregate poverty statistic that is the end product, then a certain amount of approximation may be acceptable. There does not have to be the fineness of classification necessary to ensure equity in the payment of benefits. Members of Parliament will not find their constituents complaining because they have been left out of the poverty total!

Second, it may be possible to identify common ground even where there is not complete agreement. People may prefer an imperfect measure to one that matches their ideal in all respects. They may agree that the poverty line for a single person should be at least £X a week, even if they do not agree how much higher it should be. We may, therefore, set an official standard which the majority regard as too low, but which very few regard as too high. In his assessment of the US poverty line, Joseph Kershaw said that 'it worked' because 'although the definition undoubtedly classifies some poor people as nonpoor, it classifies very few nonpoor as poor. Objections are raised from time to time, but rarely does anyone assert that ... any appreciable number of those counted as poor are really nonpoor'.[20] What is more, the simplicity of a '50 per cent of average income' criterion is positively an advantage in terms of transparency when it comes to public debate.

Third, one of the objects of the *Poverty Report* is to divert attention from a single number. The report should present a range of information, as well as an informed commentary. The range will no doubt include different poverty cut-offs: the US Bureau of the Census shows people living at 50, 75, 125, 150 and 175 per cent of the official poverty line. There will be different poverty indicators (for example with different equivalence scales, or different methods of up-rating over time), just as the Bank of England publishes different inflation rates (RPIX, RPIY, and so on) in its *Inflation Report*. There will be poverty rates for different subgroups of the population, just as in the present *Households Below Average Income* publication.

Would a national poverty objective be counter-productive?

An important set of objections to the proposed *Poverty Report* and official poverty standard is that they would be counter-productive. This is a standard objection to performance targets and performance-related remuneration, and we have to ask how far it applies in the present case. The parallel is not exact, and some elements of the criticism are not relevant. For example, it is argued that performance-related pay leads individual workers not to co-operate with their peers and that it risks destroying team-work. However, this is not fully analogous: the position of individual politicians seems rather different. Cabinet colleagues may have been jealous of the political credit earned by Harold Macmillan by building 300,000 houses a year in the 1950s, but they were unlikely to have sabotaged his efforts.

The serious objection is that, as is alleged to be the case in planned economies, planning targets distort government decisions in favour of the chosen objective and against other worthy goals. The risk that the Department of Social Security would minimize the poverty statistics to the disregard of all other functions is a major ground for concern, since the objectives of social security are much broader than the alleviation of poverty. Social transfers are intended, among other considerations, to smooth income across the lifetime, to redistribute towards those with dependants, to provide for such adversities as sickness and disability, which involve a loss of income but not necessarily poverty, and to provide a general sense of security. Although it would be small protection, I would like to see the terms of reference of the *Poverty Report* include a requirement to comment where an improvement in the poverty figures had been achieved at the expense of other social goals.

A narrower version of the same objection is that, if the government is to be judged on its poverty performance, then it may concentrate on those policies which lead to improvement in the particular chosen indicator (for example, helping those who are just below the poverty line but not those more in need). This objection is epitomized by the tired joke about the Soviet nail factory which met its annual output target, set in weight, by producing a single nail. It seems to me, however, that this is less potentially serious. The risk can be moderated by careful choice of the measure, by use of multiple indicators, and by allowing the Office for National Statistics freedom to choose alternative criteria where it feels that the picture is being distorted. As Amartya Sen has emphasized, the simple head-count of poverty is inadequate, and we should employ measures which give priority to the most deprived.[21] The purpose of having a *Poverty Report*, rather than simply publication of the statistics, is that the commentary would draw attention to the limitations of the indicators and the emergence of new forms of deprivation.

The introduction of the *Poverty Report* could, alternatively, have a negative impact by crowding out substantive measures to help the poor. Is it a work-generation project for academics rather than for the unemployed? Whether this could happen depends on the constraints on government action. If the binding constraint is public expenditure, then it seems unlikely that this is a serious obstacle: the annual cost of the *Poverty Report* is unlikely to exceed £2.5 million.[22] Nor is parliamentary time likely to be a problem, since the proposal is designed in such a way that the Chancellor of the Exchequer can request the report without recourse to Parliament. The main issue is that of 'political capital', and this merges with the question of whether or not the proposal would make any difference.

Would a poverty line makeany difference?

One dismissive response to the proposal that the UK should have an official poverty line is that the Americans have had one for thirty years and it has made no difference. Indeed, the US record on anti-poverty policy is worse than that of European countries.

This dismissive view is not shared by all American observers. Among the few who have commented on this issue, the general opinion seems to be that it *does* make a difference. According to James Tobin, writing in 1970,

> the Federal war on poverty, whatever else it has accomplished, has established an official measure of the prevalence of poverty in the United States. Adoption of a specific quantitative measure, however arbitrary and debatable, will have durable and far-reaching political consequences. Administrations will be judged by their success or failure in reducing the officially measured prevalence of poverty. So long as any families are found below the official poverty line, no politician will be able to claim victory in the war on poverty or ignore the repeated solemn acknowledgements of society's obligations to its poorer members.[23]

This assessment was quoted approvingly some two decades later by Robert Haveman in his evaluation of the impact of social science research.

Nevertheless, it is an objection which one has to take seriously. The experience of the United States may not carry over to the UK. How would the establishment of a national poverty target and publication of the *Poverty Report* affect government policy towards the poor? Economists often pride themselves on not being interested in rhetoric, and may well feel that it is the substantive policy on which we should concentrate. It is not relevant what people *say* they do; all that matters is what they actually *do*. On the other hand, many non-economists believe that stated objectives are relevant, and that it may be useful to distinguish between these and the preferences which appear to underlie observed policy choices. Moreover, people may be led to change their priorities. As is noted by Amartya Sen in his essay, the role of discussion has long been recognized in the field of social choice.

In order to explore this, we need to consider the motives which influence political choices by the different actors—or the theory of political behaviour/public choice. The answer clearly depends on the model of behaviour supposed to apply to the government. Many such models have been proposed and there is little consensus as to the most appropriate. Moreover, the most appropriate model is likely to vary over space and time. Nonetheless, there is likely to be an element of 'principal/agent' in any explanation. The electorate, as 'principal', has to make choices between different manifestos in the knowledge that its 'agent', the government, will make the operative decision in the light of the information available at a subsequent date. To use a Gingrich phrase, parties are offering a 'contract'.

Viewed in principal/agent terms, there is evidently a difference between a contract written in terms of objectives and one written in form of policies. Which is preferable in terms of the final outcome is open to debate. Where there is a close link between policy and outcome, then a commitment to specific policy measures may be more effective. Suppose that voters choose between political parties each with a set of policy commitments/expectations, but after the election these commitments prove to be inconsistent with the constraints, such as those on public spending. (This situation may appear unlikely in a world where politicians are seeking to avoid any spending commitments, but a policy vacuum generates its own set of expectations.) When these conflicting commitments come to be reconciled, a specific promise to raise pensions by £Y is likely to strengthen the bargaining power of the Secretary of State for Social Security more than a generalized commitment to a national poverty performance standard. The latter can, after all, be addressed by other policy measures which do not involve public spending. But the latter argument is also the strength of the poverty performance standard. It provides grounds for raising the issue of combating poverty in all spheres of government policy. Cabinet papers from all ministers would have to include a statement as to how their proposals contribute to the reduction of poverty.

Where the links between policy measures and the ultimate goal are less clear, then the case for concentrating on outcomes becomes stronger. A good example is provided by the long-standing debate over means-tested benefits.[24] Some people see these as an efficient way of targeting help to the poor; others (myself included) regard them as unsatisfactory on account of their stigmatizing characteristics and the seriously incomplete take-up. If, however, both sides are agreed on the objective, and the government is committed to such a target, then this provides the basis for assessing different policy mechanisms as their effectiveness becomes clearer.

Why should a government accept a performance target?

Touching on the theory of economic policy brings us to the fourth objection. Why should any political party accept a prior constraint on its actions? There are several possible reasons. It could be concerned with internal party dynamics, as with Gingrich's Contract with America; or it could be to do with external credibility, as with the Conservative government's adoption of the inflation target after the UK left the Exchange Rate Mechanism; or it could involve credibility with the electorate. It is the third of these that I consider here, in the context of a highly simplified model of the choice of political platforms.[25]

Suppose that there are two political parties concerned both with being in power and with achieving their interests, which are different for the two parties. In order to dramatise the situation, suppose that one party, L, has a preference for a state-transfer programme and that the other, C, believes that the best level of state spending is zero. Suppose, for the moment, that policy can be represented along the single dimension of the level of transfer spending. Voters have preferences over different levels of transfers and the implied tax rate. As far as the parties are concerned, the outcome of the election is uncertain, but the vertical axis shows the expected proportion who would favour a reduction in spending from the level shown on the horizontal axis. Each party acts as though the probability of winning is a function of the chosen policies of the two parties, and the form of the function is assumed to be such that a party can increase its chance of election by converging towards the policy of its opponent.

In such a situation, one would expect to find a convergence of political programmes, but not complete convergence. Neither political party will pursue the policy which maximizes its own objective function, since it recognizes that some compromise will increase the probability of winning the election. On the other hand, the convergence is less than complete because parties attach some weight to their own objectives. Party C will propose a transfer level less than that of party L, even though closing the gap would raise its probability of winning, since it would reduce the *value* of winning (being committed to a higher benefit level than it believes desirable).

What role would a poverty target play in these circumstances? Why should either party espouse such a target? It may appear obvious why party L would establish such a target, since it is concerned about poverty, but why should party C accept an official poverty objective, when it is opposed to state anti-poverty policy? An answer can be given in terms of credibility—just as the inflation target was introduced to ensure the credibility of economic policy after the UK left the Exchange Rate Mechanism. The description of the electoral competition assumed that political parties are pre-committed to a policy, whereas once elected they may in fact decide to follow their own preferences and not the policy on which they campaigned. If party C wins, it could then set transfers to zero, even if it had promised to maintain a certain level. If voters are rational, they take this into account, and in the limit they disregard the announced platforms. The outcome simply depends on the preferred choices of the political parties.

In such a situation, however, it may be in the interest of political parties to try to persuade voters that they will not act purely in their own interests once elected. In particular, party C may want to pre-commit itself to spend more than zero. The adoption of an official poverty line may represent a pre-commitment of this type. By announcing this target, party C may bind itself not to cut benefits, and the sophisticated electorate will therefore find it more acceptable, since it will remain closer to its campaign promises. This provides one argument why a party on the right would find it in its own interests to adopt a poverty target. Paradoxically, it is the party concerned to cut transfers which adopts the poverty target.

In the present British political context, this line of argument may appear inappropriate and unhelpful. We do not observe the Conservative Party having any evident enthusiasm for a poverty target. (Although, in parentheses, we should note how in 1970 the Conservatives made considerable play of Labour's failure to reduce child poverty; one might in the future observe an attempt by the Conservatives to steal this issue from Labour.) What about L? In the earlier analysis, party L found it in its own interest to pre-commit itself not to spend as much on benefits as it would like, and here the announcement of a poverty target may worsen rather than improve its prospects. Such a pre-commitment would simply confirm voters in their suspicions that party L would be profligate with their money. On the other hand, it is here that the decoupling of the poverty commitment from benefit spending becomes important. Policy choices are not one-dimensional, and the opening of a second front may allow additional room for manœuvre. To make no commitment is not credible, but voters may be persuaded by a commitment which is not tied to benefit spending and can be achieved by other non-transfer policies.

Finally, we should not rule out the possibility that voters too feel that they can benefit from being tied, like Ulysses, to the mast. Suppose that people have different levels of preference: higher and lower selves. One's higher self may exhibit concern for the poor, whereas one's lower self may consult only private interest. When it comes to an election one may take account only of self-interest. Recognizing our weakness, we may in this situation prefer, according to our higher selves, to be pre-committed to a policy which takes account of poverty. Put another way, the existence of an official poverty line may limit the range of policies which are put to the electorate. Voters are not exposed to temptation.

Conclusions

This essay has had an academic purpose, which is to examine a question which seems surprisingly little discussed: what would be the role of the institution of an official poverty line and the publication of an official *Poverty Report*? It has also had a missionary purpose, which is to argue the case for the UK adopting this approach. I accept that there are legitimate grounds for concern, particularly that it would focus attention on the anti-poverty function of social transfers to the exclusion of other functions, but on balance I feel that there is a good case for adopting in the UK an official poverty line which is decoupled from benefit scales and to which there is a national commitment, and for there to be an official *Poverty Report* documenting and interpreting performance in the light of this performance standard.

The Memorial Trust and Lectures

This collection helps to commemorate the life and work of Eva Colorni, who taught economics at London Guildhall University (which was then known as the City of London Polytechnic).

Five of the six essays were delivered, in their original form, as Eva Colorni Memorial Lectures at the University. The exception is Amartya Sen's introductory essay on social commitment and democracy, which was written specially for this collection.

A. B. Atkinson's lecture was delivered in autumn 1996, simultaneously with publication of this book. All the earlier lecturers were given the opportunity to make revisions. These have often been extensive. In Ronald Dworkin's case, the essay published here is in fact a new text, his memorial lecture having been delivered from notes. Paul Barker's editorial remarks are also, of course, new.

An Eva Colorni Memorial Trust, based at the University, was formed in 1985, the year of her untimely death. Its aim has been to reflect and further her belief in the possibility of social justice. Its principal activity has been to award, since 1986, annual bursaries to students of economics at London Guildhall.

The memorial lectures, under the Trust's auspices, have been part of the same commemoration. They began in 1987 (Ronald Dworkin), and continued with Albert O. Hirschman (1990), E. J. Hobsbawm (1993) and Dorothy Wedderburn (1995). Addressing general themes of social inequality and justice, they were launched at a time when the wider intellectual climate was less concerned with, and even sometimes hostile to, such a discussion. The lectures have all been given by speakers who knew Eva Colorni personally.

The author royalties from the present collection will all go to the Trust's charitable funds for future bursaries at London Guildhall University, at a time when students are under renewed financial pressure.

Eva Colorni

To teach economics was only one facet of Eva Colorni's many-sided life. She left an immediate mark on everyone who met her in her all too short life. She had great vitality and freshness. She not only loved new ideas but also had a deep curiosity and concern about people.

She had charm, generosity, great mental strength and independence, enormous practical competence, and a very Italianate, energetic beauty: star quality, you could say. She liked laughter, and disliked ceremony and convention. She loved her family, and was always at the centre of an interlocking group of friends. She was so devoted to her students that she courageously continued teaching at the City of London Polytechnic (as it then was) for a term and a half during her final illness, until the cancer that killed her at the age of 44 made this physically impossible.

She moved into new worlds all her life. As her husband, Amartya Sen, notes in his essay, she was born in wartime Italy, in 1941, into the Italian–German connection of the Colornis, Hirschmanns and Spinellis. It was a network held together by the various bonds of anti-Fascism, Jewishness, intellectuality, good looks and kinship. Politically, it was on the left. Her father was the Italian socialist philosopher Eugenio Colorni, who was killed taking part in the Resistance when she was three. Her mother, Ursula Hirschmann, was an economist, born in Berlin, who moved to Italy—then relatively non-racist—when Hitler rose to power. (Albert Hirschman is Ursula's brother.) After Eugenio's death, Ursula married his friend Altiero Spinelli, who became a leading politician. Ursula's evocative memoirs of her early life have been published under the title *Noi senzapatria*, roughly, 'Those of us who have no country'.

Eva was proud of this background, and she too moved from

country to country. After studying at Pavia University, she soon plunged into the utterly different world of India. She taught at the Delhi School of Economics. Later, she came to England. Her sister, Barbara Spinelli, has said she felt that, at the end of a life tragically cut short, Eva held to 'a mixture of Indian and European philosophy, of almost fatalistic detachment and passionate scepticism'.

But she was always, also, deeply Italian, and tremendously active. Working till dawn one summer, she created a delightful garden into which she had conveyed a large chunk of granite from the old London Bridge. The roof of her Fiat regularly had huge items strapped to it, which she had picked up in some junk shop.

She had the capacity constantly to remake her life. In 1973 she had settled in North London with Amartya Sen, who was to teach successively at the London School of Economics and Oxford. A dearly loved daughter and son were born, Indrani and Kabir. She took up her tenured post at the Polytechnic. For more than a decade, as the storm-tossed 1970s moved into the political and economic maelstrom of the 1980s, her and Amartya's house became a centre of family life, friendship and intellectual debate. She never accepted the idea of being confined to any corner of the division of labour.

She was much loved. Those who met Eva never forgot her. Their memories of her are, perhaps, her finest memorial.

PAUL BARKER

NOTES ON CONTRIBUTORS

A. B. Atkinson is the Warden of Nuffield College, Oxford University. He was previously Professor of Political Economy at Cambridge University, and Professor of Economics at the London School of Economics. He was a member of the Social Justice Commission, 1992–94. His books include *Public Economics in Action*, *Poverty and Social Security* and *Unequal Shares*.

Paul Barker is the former Editor of *New Society*. He is a writer and broadcaster, and a Senior Fellow of the Institute of Community Studies, London. Books he has edited include *The Other Britain*, *Founders of the Welfare State* and *Arts in Society*.

Ronald Dworkin is Professor of Jurisprudence, and a Fellow of University College, Oxford University, and a Professor of Law at New York University Law School. His books include *Taking Rights Seriously*, *Life's Dominion* and *Freedom's Law: The Moral Reading of the American Constitution*.

Albert O. Hirschman is Emeritus Professor of Social Science at the Institute for Advanced Study, Princeton. His books include *The Strategy of Economic Development* and *Exit, Voice and Loyalty*. The arguments in his essay—delivered in a memorial lecture in 1990—are developed more fully in his *The Rhetoric of Reaction: Perversity, Futility, Jeopardy* (Cambridge, Mass.: The Belknap Press of Harvard University Press, 1991).

E. J. Hobsbawm is Emeritus Professor of Economic and Social History, University of London. His books include *Nations and Nationalism since 1780* and the tetralogy *The Age of Revolution, The*

Age of Capital, The Age of Empire and *The Age of Extremes: The Short Twentieth Century.*

Amartya Sen is Lamont University Professor, Harvard University. He was previously Drummond Professor of Political Economy, and a Fellow of All Souls College, Oxford University. His books include *Collective Choice and Social Welfare, On Economic Inequality* and (with Jean Drèze) *Hunger and Public Action.*

Dorothy Wedderburn is a Senior Research Fellow, Imperial College, and a former Principal of Royal Holloway and Bedford New College, University of London. She is a member of an Inner London health authority. Her books include *White Collar Redundancy,* and (jointly) *The Economic Circumstances of Old People* and *Workers' Attitudes and Technology.*

NOTES TO THE ESSAYS

'Living as Equals', Paul Barker

1. Merrill D. Peterson, *Thomas Jefferson and the New Nation* (New York: Oxford University Press, 1970), 85.
2. *Prospect* (April 1996), 51.
3. For example, Winifred Hurtle in Trollope's *The Way We Live Now* (1875); see Victoria Glendenning, *Trollope* (London: Pimlico, 1993), 432.
4. Mikhail Zoshchenko, *Izbrannoe* (Ann Arbor: University of Michigan Press, 1960).
5. Matthew Cullerne Bown, *Art under Stalin* (Oxford: Phaidon, 1991), 244.
6. *Le Corbusier: Architect of the Century* (London: Arts Council of Great Britain, 1987), 174.
7. David Coleman and John Salt (eds.), *Ethnicity in the 1991 Census*, i. (London: HMSO for the Office of Population Censuses and Surveys, 1996), 247.
8. For a perceptive account of this decline, see Mark Hudson, *Coming Back Brockens: A Year in a Mining Village* (London: Jonathan Cape, 1994).
9. Jean-Jacques Servan-Schreiber, *Le Défi américain* (Paris: Denoël, 1967); translated as *The American Challenge* (London: Hamish Hamilton, 1968).
10. *Fabian Review*, 108/2 (April 1996), 1.
11. William Waldegrave, *The Binding of Leviathan: Conservatism and the Future* (London: Hamish Hamilton, 1978).
12. *Social Trends 26* (London: HMSO, 1996), table 5.18.
13. Eric Jacobs and Robert Worcester, *We British: Britain under the MORIscope* (London: Weidenfeld & Nicolson, 1990), 73.
14. Samuel Johnson, *Taxation No Tyranny* (1775).

'Social Commitment and Democracy', Amartya Sen

For helpful comments and suggestions, I am most grateful to Fabrizio Barca, Paul Barker, Carlo Boffito, Andrea Brandolini, Umberto Colombo, Renata Colorni, Albert Hirschman, Eva Monteforte, Tommaso Padoa-Schioppa, Emma Rothschild, Barbara Spinelli and Stefano Zamagni.

1. See Eugenio Colorni, *Scritti*, with an Introduction by Norberto Bobbio (Florence: La Nuova Italy, 1975); Leo Solari, *Eugenio Colorni: Ieri e oggi* (Venice: Marsilio, 1980); Altiero Spinelli, *Come ho tentato di diventare saggio* (Bologna: Il Mulino, 1984, 1987); Edmondo Paolini, *Altiero Spinelli: Appunti per una biografia* (Bologna: Il Mulino, 1988).

2. See her posthumously published autobiography, Ursula Hirschmann, *Noi senzapatria* (Bologna: Il Mulino, 1993). Her brother, Albert Hirschman, who remained close to the Italian family, was another strong influence. See also his essay on his pre-war stay in Italy and on Eugenio Colorni in his book *A Propensity to Self-Subversion* (Cambridge, Mass.: Harvard University Press, 1995), ch. 9: 'Doubts and Anti-Fascist Actions in Italy, 1936–1938'.

3. On this see Tommaso Padoa-Schioppa, *The Road to Monetary Union in Europe* (Oxford: Clarendon Press, 1994), 8.

4. For philosophical as well as economic arguments for a basic income and related policies, see Philippe Van Parijs, *Real Freedom for All: What (if Anything) Can Justify Capitalism?* (Oxford: Clarendon Press, 1995). On the case for subsidies to raise employment and to reduce poverty, see Edmund S. Phelps, *The Social Wage* (Cambridge, Mass.: Harvard University Press, forthcoming). See also the proposals in J.-P. Fitoussi and R. Rosanvallon, *Le Nouvel Age des inégalités* (Paris: Seuil, 1996), and also another approach briefly identified by A. B. Atkinson, 'The Case for a Participation Income', *Political Quarterly* 67 (1996), 67–70.

5. I examined some of the issues involved in my talk to the Umberto and Elisabetta Mauri Scuola for booksellers, in Venice on 26 January 1996, which has been published in Italian in *il Mulino* 364 (1996), 199–216.

6. See John Dewey and J. H. Tufts, *Ethics* (New York: Holt, 1932), 175. This perspective provides a fruitful approach to practical ethics in general. For some technical issues involved in such conflicts, see Isaac Levi, *Hard Choices* (Cambridge: Cambridge University Press, 1986), and Amartya Sen, *On Ethics and Economics* (Oxford: Blackwell, 1987).

7. These issues are discussed in Jean Drèze and Amartya Sen, *Hunger and Public Action* (Oxford: Clarendon Press, 1989), and *India: Economic*

Development and Social Opportunity (Delhi: Oxford University Press, 1995).

8. Acceptance speech at the award ceremony for the second Senator Giovanni Agnelli International Prize in 1990 ('Individual Freedom as a Social Commitment'), published by the Agnelli Foundation, and also in the *New York Review of Books*, 14 June 1990.

9. I have tried to discuss the underlying ethical issues in 'Well-being, Agency and Freedom: The Dewey Lectures 1984', *Journal of Philosophy*, 82 (April 1985).

10. This is also discussed, particularly in the context of the poorer economies, in 'Human Development and Financial Conservatism', my keynote address at the International Conference on Financing Human Resource Development, arranged by the Asian Development Bank, on 17 November 1995; to be published in the *Asian Economic Review*.

11. Michael Bruno, 'Inflation, Growth and Monetary Control: Nonlinear Lessons from Crisis and Recovery', text of Paolo Baffi Lecture at the Bank of Italy, 1995.

12. Felix Rohatyn, the financial expert and entrepreneur, summed up the contemporary situation thus: 'The country's financial situation is very strong. Over the last three years, as a result of the Clinton Administration's fiscal policies and the Federal Reserve's monetary policies, the budget deficit has been cut in half, to less than 2.5 per cent of the gross domestic product. Interest rates have decreased significantly, and the Dow Jones industrial average is near an all-time high. In addition our trade deficit is coming down, and the dollar has strengthened. Even though the economy is slowing down, this is not the stuff of financial crisis.' (Felix Rohatyn, ' "Budget Crisis" Defined', *New York Times*, Sunday 14 January 1996, Op-Ed, p. 13.)

13. In his essay in this volume, 'Promise and Performance: Why We Need an Official *Poverty Report*', A. B. Atkinson argues powerfully for the importance of having systematic reports on poverty, along with a clear definition of the national poverty line.

14. For very different perspectives on the idea of such a 'natural rate', see, in defence of it, Edmund S. Phelps, *Structural Slumps* (Cambridge, Mass.: Harvard University Press, 1993), and in opposition to it, Luigi L. Pasinetti, *Structural Economic Dynamics* (Cambridge: Cambridge University Press, 1993), and Robert Eisner, *The Misunderstood Economy* (Boston, Mass.: Harvard Business School Press, 1994).

15. Edmund S. Phelps, 'God, Marx and the "Natural Rate"', *Wall Street Journal*, 5 May 1994.

16. When the 'budget constraint' can be explicitly specified (involving the maximally acceptable deficit), the real 'cost' can be expressed technically as the so-called 'Lagrangean multiplier' associated with that constraint, reflecting the value of a unit of budgetary spending at the margin. For a more ambitious exercise, the value of expanding the budget constraint has to be compared with the costs generated by it, including the factors already specified.

17. The pioneering move came from Kenneth J. Arrow, *Social Choice and Individual Values* (New York: Wiley, 1951; 2nd edn., 1963). There was a very rapid expansion of the literature in the 1970s and 1980s, in which I have also been personally much involved; see, for example, *Collective Choice and Social Welfare* (San Francisco, Calif.: Holden-Day, 1971; republished, Amsterdam: North-Holland, 1979); and *Choice, Welfare and Measurement* (Oxford: Blackwell, and Cambridge, Mass.: MIT Press, 1982). It is a subject in which Eva took an active interest, and I had the privilege of discussing some of the foundational issues in social choice theory with her (the latter book was also dedicated to Eva).

18. Critical reviews of the technical literature can be found in Kotaro Suzumura, *Rational Choice, Collective Decisions and Social Welfare* (Cambridge: Cambridge University Press, 1983); Prasanta Pattanaik and Maurice Salles, *Social Choice and Welfare* (Amsterdam: North-Holland, 1983); and my 'Social Choice Theory', in K. J. Arrow and M. Intriligator (eds.), *Handbook of Mathematical Economics* (Amsterdam: North-Holland, 1986). See also the journal *Social Choice and Welfare*, which includes papers on more recent works.

19. Frank Knight, *Freedom and Reform* (New York: Harper, 1947), 280.

20. James M. Buchanan, 'Social Choice, Democracy, and Free Markets', *Journal of Political Economy*, 62 (1954), 120.

21. Michael Bruno, *Crisis, Stabilization, and Economic Reform: Therapy by Consensus* (Oxford: Clarendon Press, 1993).

22. I have tried to discuss the general issues involved in participatory solutions to social problems in my Presidential Address to the American Economic Association, 'Rationality and Social Choice', published in *American Economic Review*, 85 (1995).

23. Tommaso Padoa-Schioppa, *The Road to Monetary Union in Europe* (Oxford: Clarendon Press, 1994), 22.

24. Studies like those of Edmund S. Phelps, *The Social Wage*, and Jean-Paul Fitoussi and R. Rosanvallon, *Le Nouvel Age des inégalités*, referred to earlier, point in the directions in which we have to look to overcome chronic problems of unemployment and low-wage work. There is need to go well beyond purely macroeconomic policy, and to supplement aggregative approaches with programmes that influence relative prices and costs, and the incentive to hire rather than fire.

25. The extraordinarily high ratio of resource use in military expenditure, even in very poor countries, is reported in some detail in UNDP, *Human Development Report 1994* (New York: UNDP, 1994).

26. Sir Michael Atiyah, President of the Royal Society, 'Anniversary Address', at the Anniversary Meeting of the Royal Society on 30 November 1995.

'Do Liberty and Equality Conflict?', Ronald Dworkin

1. This account of interpretation is further explained and defended in my book *Law's Empire* (Cambridge, Mass.: Harvard University Press, 1986).

2. I describe a variety of objections to welfare-based conceptions of distributive justice in 'What is Equality? Part 1: Equality of Welfare', *Philosophy and Public Affairs* (1981).

3. See 'What is Equality? Part 2: Equality of Resources', *Philosophy and Public Affairs* (1981).

4. Robert Nozick made this point particularly effectively in his book *Anarchy, State and Utopia* (Basic Books, 1976), 161–3.

5. The details of such a scheme are provided in 'What is Equality? Part 2'.

6. As I just suggested, such redistributive policies need not take the form only of monetary welfare payments. In fact equality of resources prefers, so far as this is consistent with the hypothetical insurance model, provision of opportunities, particularly of jobs, to the provision of funds. Providing jobs, though perhaps more expensive than providing money transfers, better insures that people will have only the income they are prepared to work to produce, which is part of equality's goal.

7. See Isaiah Berlin, 'Two Concepts of Liberty', in his collection *Four Essays on Liberty* (Oxford: Oxford University Press, 1969), 128.

8. I am here assuming that appealing to equality of resources could not justify putting some people, in an unequal society, in a worse position than they are and worse than the position they would have if equality

of resources were fully realized, just in order to improve equality on balance or overall. For a defence of that assumption, see 'What is Equality? Part 3: The Place of Equality' in *Iowa Law Review*, 73 (1987), 1–54.

9. This heated and complex issue is discussed at length in my recent book, *Freedom's Law: The Moral Reading of the American Constitution* (Cambridge, Mass.: Harvard University Press, 1996), part 2.

'Two Hundred Years of Reactionary Rhetoric', Albert O. Hirschman

1. 'Citizenship and Social Class', Alfred Marshall Lectures given in Cambridge in 1949, reprinted in T. H. Marshall, *Class, Citizenship, and Social Development* (New York: Doubleday, 1965), ch. 4.

2. Alfred N. Whitehead, *Symbolism: Its Meaning and Effect* (New York: Capricorn Books, 1926, 1959), 88.

3. Jean Starobinski, 'La Vie et les aventures du mot "réaction" ', *Modern Language Review*, 70 (1975), pp. xxi–xxxi.

4. F. Brunot, *Histoire de la langue française, des origines à 1900* (Paris: Colin, 1905–53), vol. 9, part 2, 843–4.

5. For a broad survey of perverse effects by a sociologist, see Raymond Boudon, *Effets pervers et order social* (Paris: Presses Universitaires de France, 1977).

6. J. J. Ampère, *Mélanges d'histoire littéraire*, ii (Paris, 1877), 323. The passage here quoted is reproduced from a review written in 1856. See also Richard Herr, *Tocqueville and the Old Regime* (Princeton, N.J.: Princeton University Press, 1962), 108–9.

7. François Furet, *Penser la Révolution française* (Paris: Gallimard, 1978), 31.

8. Gaetano Mosca, *The Ruling Class* (Elementi di scienza politica), ed. and introduced by Arthur Livingston (New York: McGraw Hill, 1939), p. x.

9. Ibid. 284–5.

10. Mosca, 'Teorica dei governi e governo parlamentare', in *Scritti politici*, ed. Giorgio Sola (Turin: UTET, 1982), i. 476; translation adapted from James H. Meisel, *The Myth of the Ruling Class* (Ann Arbor, Mich.: University of Michigan Press, 1958), 106. Emphasis in the original.

11. Mosca, 'Teorica', 478. Emphasis in original.

12. Richard Bellamy, *Modern Italian Social Theory* (Stanford, Calif.: Stanford University Press, 1987), 40–1.
13. Vilfredo Pareto, *Cours d'économie politique,* ed. G. H. Bousquet and Giovanni Busino (Geneva: Droz, 1964), para. 1054.
14. Ibid., para. 1055.
15. Ibid., para. 1056.
16. Vilfredo Pareto, 'La Courbe de la répartition de la richesse' (1896), re-published in Pareto, *Écrits sur la courbe de la répartition de la richesse,* ed. and introduced by Giovanni Busino (Geneva: Droz, 1965), 1–15.
17. Pareto, *Écrits sur la courbe,* introduction by Busino, p. x.
18. Ibid. 17.
19. *Journal of Law and Economics,* 13 (April 1976), 1–10.
20. Robert E. Goodin and Julian LeGrand, *Not Only the Poor: The Middle Classes and the Welfare State* (London: Allen & Unwin, 1987).
21. Leszek Kolakowski, *Towards a Marxist Humanism* (New York: Grove Press, 1968), 152–3.

'Are All Tongues Equal?', E. J. Hobsbawm

1. Guy Hermet, *Histoire des nations et du nationalisme en Europe* (Paris: Le Seuil, 1996), 115.
2. Elie Kedourie, *Nationalism* (London: Hutchinson, 1960), 76.
3. Frida Thórarinsdóttir, *Nation, State and Language: An Invented Unity* (New York: New School for Social Research, Center for Studies of Social Change, working paper no. 188, 1994), 28–30.
4. E. J. Hobsbawm, *Nations and Nationalism since 1780: Programme, Myth, Reality* (Cambridge: Cambridge University Press, 1991), 103 .
5. S. Thernstrom *et al.* (eds.), *Harvard Encyclopedia of American Ethnic Groups* (Cambridge, Mass.: Harvard University Press, 1980), 632.
6. Hugh Seton-Watson, *Nations and States* (London: Methuen, 1977), 182.
7. Joshua Fishman, 'Language Maintenance', in S.Thernstrom *et al.* (eds.), *Harvard Encyclopedia of American Ethnic Groups,* 636.
8. See Björn Jernudd and Michael Shapiro (eds.), *The Politics of Language Purism* (Berlin and New York: Mouton de Gruyter, 1989), 218.
9. Paul Robert Magocsi, 'The Birth of a New Nation or the Return of an Old Problem? The Rusyns of East Central Europe', *Canadian Slavonic Papers/Revue canadienne des slavistes,* 34/3 (Sept. 1992), 199–223.

'The Superiority of Collective Action', Dorothy Wedderburn

1. T. H. Marshall, *Sociology at the Cross Roads* (London: Heinemann, 1963).
2. For a review of the background and the early years of the NHS see C. Webster, *The Health Service since the War*, i. *Problems of Health Care* (London: HMSO, 1988).
3. M. Foot, *Aneurin Bevan*, ii. *1945–1960* (St Albans: Paladin, 1975).
4. B. Abel-Smith, *The Cost of the National Health Service* (Cambridge: Cambridge University Press, 1956).
5. For a stimulating analysis of the development of the NHS see R. Klein, *The Politics of the National Health Service*, 2nd edn. (London: Longman, 1989).
6. *Royal Commission on the National Health Service* (London: HMSO, 1979).
7. Secretary of State for Health *et al.*, *Working for Patients* (London: HMSO, 1989).
8. DHSS, *Inequalities in Health: Report of a Working Group* (London: HMSO, 1980).
9. Department of Health, *Variation in Health: What Can the Department of Health and the NHS Do?* (1995).
10. J. Hills, 'Health Services' in *The Future of Welfare* (York: Joseph Rowntree Foundation, 1993).
11. Social and Community Planning Research, *British Social Attitudes: Cumulative Sourcebook* (Aldershot: Gower, 1992).
12. B. Abel-Smith, *How to Contain Health Care Costs: An International Dilemma* (University of London, 1994).
13. Joseph Rowntree Foundation, *Inquiry into Income and Wealth* (York: Joseph Rowntree Foundation, 1995).
14. R. Wilkinson, 'Health, Redistribution and Growth' in A. Glyn and D. Miliband (eds.), *Paying for Inequality* (London: IPPR/Rivers Oram Press, 1994).

'Promise and Performance', A. B. Atkinson

I am grateful to Amartya Sen and Paul Barker for their most helpful comments.

1. I say 'in the United Kingdom' since I should make clear at the outset that I am considering poverty in rich countries. This is very different

from poverty on a world scale. It could well be argued that poverty in Africa and Asia is so important as to preclude any consideration of the deprived within OECD countries. Although it is my own personal judgement that world poverty has *priority*, I do not accept that this leaves no room for consideration of poverty in the UK.

2. 'Inflation Report', *Bank of England Quarterly Bulletin* (Feb. 1993), 3.

3. W. H. Beveridge, *Social Insurance and Allied Services*, Cmd. 6404 (London: HMSO, 1942), 14.

4. John Veit Wilson, 'Memorandum, House of Commons Social Services Committee, Minimum Income' (London: HMSO, 1989), 85.

5. See Brian Abel-Smith and Peter Townsend, *The Poor and the Poorest* (London: Bell, 1965); and A. B. Atkinson, *Poverty in Britain and the Reform of Social Security* (Cambridge: Cambridge University Press, 1969). The assistance standard was applied for a number of years in the official studies of low-income families, which examined how many people had incomes below the Supplementary Benefit scale or within a certain percentage of that scale—see *Low Income Families 1985* (London: Department of Health and Social Security, 1988).

6. *Hansard* (14 July 1983), cols. 1018–19 and 1022.

7. Commission of the European Communities, *Interim Report on a Specific Community Action Programme to Combat Poverty* (Brussels: European Commission, 1989), 9.

8. This quotation is from page 9 of G. M. Fisher, 'The Development and History of the Poverty Thresholds', *Social Security Bulletin*, 55/4 (1992), 3–46. The reference to Orshansky's work is 'Counting the Poor: Another Look at the Poverty Profile', *Social Security Bulletin*, 28 (1965), 3–29.

9. US Bureau of the Census, *Poverty in the United States: 1992* (Washington, DC: US Government Printing Office, 1993), p. viii.

10. Committee on Ways and Means, *US House of Representatives Green Book* (Washington, DC: US Government Printing Office, 1992), 637 and 798.

11. The new framework for monetary policy is described by Mervyn King, 'Monetary Policy', *Fiscal Studies*, 15 (1994), 109–28. For discussion of inflation targets in other countries, see Leonardo Leiderman and Lars Svensson (eds.), *Inflation Targets* (London: Centre for Economic Policy Research, 1995).

12. I am referring to the UK, but the argument may well apply to other OECD countries, with appropriate institutional modifications.

13. Like many innovations in the UK, a *Poverty Report* was first conceived (in 1969) by Michael Young, and reports were published in the 1970s: M. Young (ed.), *Poverty Report 1974* (London: Temple Smith, 1974); M. Young (ed.), *Poverty Report 1975* (London: Temple Smith, 1975); P. Willmott (ed.), *Sharing Inflation: Poverty Report 1976* (London: Temple Smith, 1976). The publications of the Child Poverty Action Group performed much the same function and attracted considerable political attention: see Frank Field, *Poverty and Politics* (London: Heinemann, 1982).

14. The US Bureau of the Census publishes extensive material on the standard errors of its estimates, and comments on the statistical significance of changes.

15. *Households Below Average Income 1979–1992/93* (London: Department of Social Security, 1995).

16. John Veit Wilson, *Dignity Not Poverty: A Minimum Income Standard for the UK*, Commission on Social Justice Issue Paper 6 (London: IPPR, 1994), 35.

17. Jan Tinbergen, *On the Theory of Economic Policy* (Amsterdam: North Holland, 1952), and *Centralization and Decentralization in Economic Policy* (Amsterdam: North Holland, 1954).

18. Jean Drèze and Amartya Sen, *Hunger and Public Action* (Oxford: Clarendon Press, 1989).

19. A. B. Atkinson, Karin Gardiner, Valerie Lechêne, and Holly Sutherland, 'Comparing Poverty in France and the United Kingdom', Welfare State Programme Discussion Paper 84 (London: LSE, 1993).

20. J. A. Kershaw, *Government Against Poverty* (Washington, DC: Brookings Institution, 1970), 13.

21. Amartya Sen, 'Poverty: An Ordinal Approach to Measurement', *Econometrica*, 44 (1976), 219–31.

22. The reported cost of the first report of the Royal Commission on the Distribution of Income and Wealth in 1975 was £124,300.

23. James Tobin, 'Raising the Incomes of the Poor', in K. Gordon (ed.), *Agenda for the Nation* (Washington, DC: Brookings Institution, 1970), 83. See also Robert Haveman, *Poverty Policy and Poverty Research* (Madison: University of Wisconsin Press, 1987).

24. By means-tested benefits, I mean those subject to a test of current income and a test of assets.

25. The model is based on that of two-party competition described by Alberto Alesina, 'Credibility and Policy Convergence in a Two-Party

System with Rational Voters', *American Economic Review*, 78 (1988), 796–805. The model here is a development of that in A. B. Atkinson, 'The Institution of an Official Poverty Line and Economic Policy', STICERD Welfare State Programme Discussion Paper WSP/98 (London: LSE, 1993).

INDEX